THE GUIDE TO
MYSTERIOUS ARRAN

THE GUIDE TO
MYSTERIOUS ARRAN

GEOFF HOLDER

The
History
Press

In memory of Bill Jones, mountaineer and good bloke.
'Hob-gob-shelob-delob.'

First published in 2008 by The History Press

Reprinted 2008, 2011, 2013

The History Press
The Mill, Brimscombe Port,
Stroud, Gloucestershire, GL5 2QG
www.thehistorypress.co.uk

British Library Cataloguing in Publication Data.
A catalogue record for this book is available from the British Library.

ISBN 978 0 7524 4720 9

Typesetting and origination by The History Press Ltd.
Printed in Great Britain

CONTENTS

ACKNOWLEDGEMENTS

I would like to thank: Bill Caswell, custodian at Brodick Castle, for kindly showing me around and sharing Beckfordiana; Stuart Gough, archivist of the Arran Heritage Museum, for allowing access to the archive and ferreting out juicy specimens; the staff of the Local Studies section of AK Bell Library, Perth, for their usual forbearance; Nick Underdown and the *Arran Voice* for assistance; Carol Primrose and Maureen Smith for sharing their stories; Robin Bell, manager of Arran Distillery; John Wilson, for having the perfect writer's Arran bolthole at Tim's Barn; the various Arranachs who picked me up when hitching around the island; Messrs J.A. Balfour and W.M. MacKenzie, for editing the two volumes of *The Book of Arran* in 1910 and 1914 respectively, without which this work would have been all the poorer; Paul Revell, for website wizardry; Jenni Wilson, for designing the map; my editor, Cate Ludlow, for her enthusiasm and dedication to the cause; Shade, for canine companionship on long walks beset with mud and rain; Slick, for feline friendship on late-night laptop vigils; and Ségolène Dupuy, for digital magic, driving and general Ségolène-ness, as well as for a memorable and muddy wheelchair visit to Machrie Moor.

Unless otherwise stated, all photographs are by the author.

For more information visit www.geoffholder.co.uk.

The Calmac Ferry at Brodick with the peak of Goatfell in the background.

INTRODUCTION

This guide tells you about the strange, the odd and the mysterious on Arran – everything from witchcraft, folk magic, ghosts and fairies, to graveyards, ancient archaeological sites dealing with the dead and the gods, and modern curiosities in the landscape. Here too you'll find legends and myths, customs and beliefs, and various forms of eccentric behaviour.

In several senses, Arran is a borderland. It stands between the Lowlands and the Highlands, between the historically Anglophone central Scottish mainland and the Gaelic west. Geographically it is a Hebridean island, but politically it has usually fallen within the sphere of influence of the Lowlands. This means that for centuries it was a contested area, between Scots and the Vikings, and between the Scottish monarchy and their enemies such as the Lords of the Isles and others. The Highland Boundary Geological Fault runs midway through the island, so it is, geologically speaking, both Lowland and Highland. It was also a transition zone for society, being one of the last places where absolute aristocratic rule prevailed – a satirical mention in an early twentieth century Glasgow newspaper noted that, 'The first cuckoo of Spring was heard yesterday on Arran, by kind permission of his Grace the Duke of Hamilton' – before giving way to mass tourism and democratic administration. In terms of weather it is an island of two coasts, the west often having a different day to the east. And it is a borderland between Gaelic folk belief and contemporary rationalism, between the supernatural realm and the modern mundane world – encounters with fairies, for example, have been reported on the island not just in the past, but also in the twenty-first century.

Borderlands are liminal places. Liminality is a key concept in dealing with magic and the supernatural. Liminality is that which is betwixt and between, a transition, a threshold. A liminal time or place can either make a supernatural event more likely to occur, or it can provide the right conditions to make an act of magic more powerful. Liminal times are typically dusk and midnight, as well as dates such as Hallowe'en, Hogmanay, the solstices and equinoxes, and Beltane (1 May). Liminal places include caves, bogs, rivers, parish or estate boundaries, and the area between high and low water mark.

This book covers the following topics:

Encounters with non-human entities – not just ghosts and fairies, but also angels, bocans (malign spirits), urisks (hairy anthropoid creatures, similar to Bigfoot but endowed with language) and selkies (seals who can transform into humans).

Death and the afterlife – this includes graveyards, tombstones and prehistoric burial sites.

Religious phenomena such as miracles, holy wells and saints, as well as prehistoric ritual monuments (stone circles, standing stones and the like).

Mythical characters like Fingal and his family, and Celtic gods.

Legends that have accrued to real-life characters such as Robert the Bruce.

Witchcraft and all kinds of magic.

Folklore (defined as broadly as you wish).

Carved stones and other strange and marvellous sculpture.

The book is organised geographically. You can find everything mysterious and weird about one location in the same place and the text flows logically with the traveller in mind. Walking directions are given for many of the places mentioned, particularly hard-to-find prehistoric sites. The first chapter starts with Brodick and proceeds in a broadly clockwise route around the island. Cross-references to other locations are shown in CAPS. Things worth seeing are asterisked, from ★ to ★★★.

A FEW KEY CONCEPTS

Apotropaic. Protective against evil. The word can apply to charms, amulets, rituals, or elements such as rowan trees, salt, oatmeal, iron and so on.

Magical Thinking. This is a mental process that underlies folk magic, charms and witchcraft. For example, certain things, such as a saint's relics, water from a special source, or an unusual stone, are regarded as possessing power. This power can be accessed either through proximity to the source, usually by touching it (or by being buried close to a saint's grave), or through transfer – for instance, if a stone of power is placed in water, that water obtains some of the power. Further, the notion of 'sympathetic magic' allows that things which have been connected once are connected for ever – so a hair taken from a cow, or that cow's milk, can be used to curse that specific cow.

Simulacra. Natural formations in trees and rocks which we, pattern-seeking apes that we are, interpret as faces, animals and signs from God.

Storytelling. Our species is misnamed – *Homo sapiens* (wise human) should be *Pan narrans*, the storytelling ape. It is in our nature to take a chaotic series of events and turn it into a story. We do it all the time in our daily lives. Paranormal events are often random and confusing, but they quickly become transformed into a ghost story. Moral: don't depend on stories if you're looking for truth.

'**Tradition**'. Also known as 'it is said that', 'they say that', and other get-outs used by writers to bring a spurious gravitas to tall tales. Treat with caution.

'**Truth**'. Just because a respected chronicler from a previous age has written something down, doesn't make it true. And I'm often reporting the words of storytellers, fantasists, liars and journalists. *Caveat lector.*

THE PHYSICAL SETTING AND GETTING AROUND

Arran is a spectacularly beautiful island with a mountainous massif in the north sloping down via a high moorland plateau to lower agricultural land in the far south. Most of the 5,000 population lives on the east coast, in Brodick, Lamlash and Whiting Bay. Communities elsewhere are small and scattered. Communications are limited. The A841 circumnavigates the island, and there are two high-level cross-island roads, The String and The Ross. The main road is frequently narrow and beset by tight bends and blind corners. Do not expect to speed. If you are not bringing a car, pick up the bus timetable. The buses cover the whole of the island and meet every ferry,

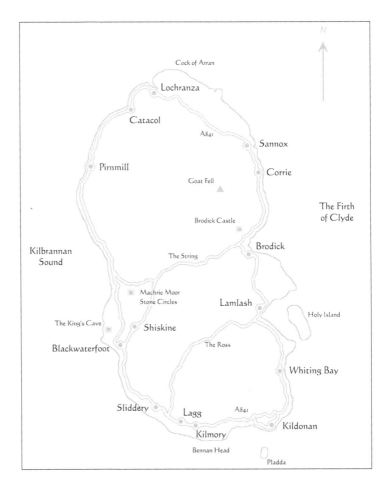

The Isle of Arran.

but if you are trying to visit more than one location in a day you may find yourself wishing that the buses were rather more frequent. Arran is of course a walkers' paradise, and consequently there are numerous walking guides available. I have found Paddy Dillon's *Walking on the Isle of Arran* to be very useful. If you don't want to trek off into the mountains there are still many low-level forestry walks as well as the Isle of Arran Coastal Way, which follows a continuous 62 mile (100km) path around the island. The walk can be done in small sections and for my money is an easy way to access some of the best and most varied scenery on Arran, although at times the signposting is incomplete or just plain confusing. A guidebook is available, although again I'd not trust absolutely everything it says. The high peaks of Arran are as exposed and dangerous as any other Scottish mountains, and, even on low-level walks, you should be prepared for boggy conditions, rain (lots of rain) and mud (ditto), whatever the season. I personally find that – such is the extent of mud in some areas during times of heavy rainfall – Wellingtons will serve you better than walking boots. The best map for walking, exploring and finding sites is the Ordnance Survey 1:25000 Explorer, number 361. Having it waterproofed is a jolly good idea.

There are over a hundred caves on Arran. Some are well known and relatively easy to access; others are little-visited and challenging to explore. If venturing into any cave, take a torch and have due regard for your own safety – most of the caves are pitch dark, uneven underfoot, and dirty and slippery. Note that some sea caves may be cut off by a high tide.

THE SCOTTISH OUTDOOR ACCESS CODE

Everyone has the right to be on most land and inland water providing they act responsibly. Your access rights and responsibilities are explained fully in the Scottish Outdoor Access Code. Find out more by visiting www.outdooraccess-scotland.com or telephoning your local Scottish Natural Heritage office.

The key things are to:

Take responsibility for your own actions
Respect the interests of other people
Care for the environment

Access rights can be exercised over most of Scotland, from urban parks and path networks to our hills and forests, and from farmland and field margins to our beaches, lochs and rivers. However, access rights don't apply everywhere, such as in buildings or their immediate surroundings, or in houses or their gardens, or most land in which crops are growing.

Some sites in this book are near houses and other private property; always ask permission – it's simple good manners. Don't disturb animals (wild or domestic). Respect the sites – do not scrape away lichen, leave offerings, do any damage or drop litter (even better, pick litter up – it's good karma).

GEOLOGY

It can be argued that geology as a modern science was born on Arran, when in 1787 James Hutton identified an unconformity, a site where rocks of widely different ages lie together at varying angles. Hutton's *Theory of the Earth* showed that over millions of years mountains were continually being uplifted and eroded – he has rightly been called 'the father of geological time'. Arran remains a magnet for geologists, as it contains so many different rocks and features. Even for the non-specialist, many of these are of great scenic interest. The south coast has hundreds of linear rock walls called dykes, made of igneous material that has resisted erosion. From viewpoints such as BENNAN HEAD these 'dyke swarms' are a spectacular sight. During the Ice Age the island had its own ice cap, and the corries and U-shaped valleys of the mountain range owe their shape to the grinding power of the ice. When the glaciers eventually melted, the reduction in weight caused Arran to rise up, creating the raised beaches which are another characteristic aspect of the scenery. The large granite boulders that dot the coast (such as CLACH A' CHATH) are glacial erratics, transported from the mountains and left high and dry when the ice retreated. A number of these supplied some of the boulders used in the stone circles on MACHRIE MOOR, while other circles and standing stones were derived from another distinctive Arran rock, red sandstone.

Machrie Moor
stone circles,
Circle 2.

ARCHAEOLOGY

Many a wild and weird tradition hovers over these old monuments. (John McArthur, *The Antiquities of Arran*)

It's virtually impossible to walk anywhere in Arran without bumping into some reminder of the past, whether it is prehistoric sites or the remains of abandoned nineteenth-century villages.

The temporary campsites of Mesolithic (very roughly, 8000-4000BC) nomadic hunter-gatherers have been identified at Auchareoch, Machrie (Balnagore), Kildonan and Glenshurig, although there is nothing to see. At this period all but the highest peaks were covered in forest. The key archaeological sites of the Neolithic period (approximately 4,000-2,000BC) are the chambered cairns, usually built in a style archaeologists call 'Clyde' (as distinct from typical styles elsewhere in Scotland, such as 'Clava' or 'Orkney-Cromarty'). Arran has an exceptionally high concentration of these burial monuments, in fact the greatest number from any comparable area in Scotland; even so, the figure was still higher until comparatively recently, when agricultural clearance and a hunger for large stones for use in building bridges, roads and houses completely eliminated many cairns. Although there is great diversity among the tombs, a few features are typical. There was usually a central stone-lined chamber in which the bodies, or parts of bodies, were placed. As far as can be determined, the bodies were allowed to decay in the open air for perhaps some months, a process known as excarnation. Selected bones – typically, the skull and long bones – were then deposited in the cairns. The stones used are large and set upright. Often, several of these chambers were built in a row in what is known as a segmented gallery, with dividing septal slabs between each compartment. The entrance to the interior was marked by larger portal stones which were themselves flanked by an arc of stones forming a façade which extended out into two 'horns'. These horns formed the boundary of an open semi-circular forecourt, used for rituals in front of the monument. The chambers were roofed and then covered with a mound of earth and stones, which in some cases extended some considerable distance beyond the actual burial area, turning a grave into an impressive monumental structure. Sometimes the cairn mound was defined by a kerb of stones, and occasionally secondary burial chambers were inserted into the mound. The sheer effort involved in moving and placing the megalithic stones and building the mounds, and the archaeological evidence showing that the cairns were often used over a very long period, demonstrate the importance of rituals of death and burial to the farming communities who built these sites. None of the cairns, however, survive intact, and it's sometimes a challenge to understand the remains. The easiest to visit is TORRYLIN. Other popular sites include the GIANTS' GRAVES and MEALLACH'S GRAVE, and fine examples can also be seen at SANNOX and EAST BENNAN. In many cases the cairns are in very atmospheric locations.

From the late Neolithic (around 2500BC) through the Bronze Age (about 2000-400BC) standing stones and stone circles were erected, clearly for ritual and religious purposes. Many of these mysterious and magnificent monuments still stand – at the very least AUCHENGALLON, AUCHENCAR and, especially, MACHRIE MOOR, should not be missed, while there are many other excellent sites, including single stones, stone pairs, 'four-poster' stone circles (which have, as the name suggests, a typical rectangular arrangement of four stones) and other circles. Variants are the 'ring-cairn', in which a central burial cairn mound has been encircled by a ring of standing stones, and the 'kerb-cairn', where the surrounding ring forms a continuous kerb. Generally speaking, in contrast to the communal burials of the Neolithic, the typical Bronze Age burial was individual, either in a small stone-lined grave called a cist (pronounced 'kist') or as a cremation. Some cists are found inserted into the mounds of earlier Neolithic cairns, while stone circles often had a small number of associated cist or cremation burials. A very small number of standing stones bear cupmarks, enigmatic circular depressions carved for purposes unknown by prehistoric peoples. Arran does have one truly spectacular example of prehistoric rock art, the cornucopia of cup-and-ring marks on a sheet of bedrock at STRONACH in Glenshurig.

Iron Age (*c.* 400BC-AD40) structures are best represented by hill forts, the largest of which is DRUMADOON, and duns, small fortified homesteads, such as at TORR A CHAISTEAL and KINGSCROSS. There are no Roman monuments on Arran, and later peoples only come into vague focus with the Pictish carvings in the KING'S CAVE, the works of the Celtic saints of the Dark Ages (see ST MOLAISE'S CAVE) and the Vikings (see ST MOLAISE'S CAVE, KINGSCROSS and LAMLASH).

The giants of the early archaeological investigations on Arran were James Bryce, who in 1861 dug five stone circles on MACHRIE MOOR in just one day, and J.A. Balfour and Thomas Bryce, who between them excavated numerous sites in the early twentieth century. Balfour went on to edit the first volume of *The Book of Arran*. Although their methods were crude by modern standards and many of their interpretations are now outdated, they still stand as pioneers. Much more on Arran's archaeological sites can be found on the online 'Canmore' database of the Royal Commission on the Ancient and Historical Monuments of Scotland, www.rcahms. gov.uk, and the Sites and Monuments Record of the West of Scotland Archaeology Service, www.wosas.org.uk. Both these websites are invaluable, and have formed the background for much of what is written about the archaeological sites in this book. A much more informal view can be obtained from the personal entries on www.the-modernantiquarian.com, the community of megalith fans that has mushroomed from Julian Cope's books *The Modern Antiquarian* and *The Megalithic European*.

POST-PREHISTORIC CHRONOLOGY

Sixth century onwards – Arran occupied by Irish Gaels of the Dal Riata.

AD590 (approx) – St Molaise active on Holy Island.

c. 800 – Vikings occupy Arran and rule it for the next 400 years; sometime during this period a fort is built on the site of what is now Brodick Castle.

1263 – Battle of Largs. Viking (Norse) influence wanes.

1266 – Arran sold to the Scottish crown by the Norse and given to Walter Stewart.

1307 – Robert the Bruce briefly sojourns on the island.

1371 – Robert III, Stewart King of Scotland, owns Arran as his hunting ground. The identification of the island as royal property, but ill-protected and on the very limit of Scottish authority, makes it a target for enemies of the Scottish crown. Arran, through its ownership, becomes affiliated to the Lowlands, not the Islands and West Highlands. For centuries it remains as a disputed borderland between the Gaelic West and the Scots mainland.

Fifteenth century – Arran raided in turn by the English, the MacDonald Lords of the Isles, Donald Balloch, and the men of the Northern Isles.

1503 – James, Lord Hamilton, grandson of the Stewart King James II and cousin of James IV, becomes Earl of Arran, and starts to reconstruct Brodick Castle as a tower house.

Sixteenth century – Feuding erupts between the Stewarts (of the Scottish royal family) and the Hamiltons. Raids by the Campbells and the MacLeans.

1526 – The Stewarts burn Brodick Castle.

1544 – The Earl of Lennox attacks Brodick Castle.

1549 – Sir Donald Munro leaves the first (brief) traveller's description of the island.

In the first half of the seventeenth century, Brodick Castle and Arran change hands several times between the Hamiltons, the Covenanters under the Marquess of Argyll, and the Campbells.

1652 – Arran briefly occupied by Cromwell's troops. They build the artillery bastion at Brodick Castle.

1656 – The Hamiltons re-acquire Brodick Castle and much of Arran. Elevated to dukes from 1643, they effectively run Arran for the next three centuries.

1695 – Martin Martin visits the island and leaves an extensive description.

1750s – Health conscious upper-class visitors start to arrive in search of the goats' milk offered at Cladach (Brodick). Tourism, very slowly, begins.

1772 – Thomas Pennant visits Arran and leaves a detailed description that, however, is full of errors which are repeated by later writers.

Late eighteenth century – Start of massive changes in agriculture.

1807 – The Revd James Headrick writes his *Survey of Arran*. There are still no roads or bridges on the island.

1812-1815, 1821 and 1829 – The Duke of Hamilton evicts many tenants, a number of whom emigrate to Canada.

1830s – Popular tourism commences, although initially restricted by the control of the various dukes.

1840s – Most of Arran connected by roads.

Mid-nineteenth century onwards – Arran becomes a major tourist destination, especially for people from Glasgow and the industrial towns of Scotland.

1889 – The Goatfell murder.

1939-1945 – Arran is an important wartime naval base and commandos train on the island. Many aircraft crash on the mountains.

1953 – The first car ferry to Arran.

1957 – The death of the Dowager Duchess of Montrose, the last aristocratic Hamilton landowner. Brodick Castle (and later Goatfell) becomes the property of the National Trust for Scotland.

1950s – A significant fraction of the island is acquired by the Forestry Commission, who engage in massive planting of conifer plantations.

SAINTS

From the fifth century AD onwards Christian missionaries were travelling to the west of Scotland from Ireland. There are several Arran placenames which reference some of these holy men, such as Car Macholm, Columbkille, Suidhe Challum Chille and

Goatfell with Brodick Castle in the lower right.

Columba's Well (all named for St Columba, the greatest Scottish saint, also known as Colm or Columbcille); Suidhe Phadruig and Kilpatrick (both for St Patrick); Kildonan (St Donnan); and Kilbrannan Sound (St Brendan). There is however no documentary or archaeological evidence to link any of these saints with Arran, and the placenames may simply be a case of 'me too!' toponymy, borrowing the celebrity power of famous individuals to boost local status. The one Dark Ages Christian saint who has a solid connection with the island is St Molaise, for whose story see HOLY ISLAND.

VIKINGS

Throughout the Dark Ages Arran was very much part of the Gaelic world, with cultural and political links to Ireland and the Gaelic kingdom of Dal Riata on the west coast of what was to become Scotland. By the year 800, however, Arran had become a subjugated part of a Viking sea-empire that stretched from Scandinavia to Ireland. A small number of Viking graves have been found (see LAMLASH, and KINGSCROSS by WHITING BAY) and there are Norse runes in St Molaise's Cave on HOLY ISLAND. The Battle of Largs (North Ayrshire) in 1263 saw the beginning of the end of Viking domination, when, with a combination of luck, weather and tactical success, the emergent state of Scotland defeated the Vikings under Haakon of Norway. The Norse saw it rather differently, clearly blaming their defeat on the Scots' use of black magic:

The tempest that day was so furious that some vessels cut away their masts, others ran aground… Five vessels were cast ashore. So great was this storm that people said it was raised by the power of Magic, and the quantity of rain was prodigious, as is thus described. Now our deep-enquiring Sovereign encounter'd the horrid powers of enchantment, and the abominations of an impious race. The troubled flood tore many fair galleys from their moorings and swept them anchorless before its waves. A magic-raised watery tempest blew upon our warriors, ambitious of conquest, and against the floating habitations [ships] of the brave. The roaring billows and stormy blast threw shielded companies of our adventurous nation on the Scottish strand. (Sturla Þórdarson, *The Norwegian Account of Haco's Expedition Against Scotland*, 1263, translated by the Revd James Johnstone.)

Both before and after the battle the Viking fleet sheltered in Lamlash Bay. In 1266 Norway sold Arran and other islands to the Scottish crown and the Norse influence vanished – apart from the enduring legacy of language. A number of Arran's most recognisable placenames – Brodick, Lochranza, Goatfell – are Norse, and sit next to a great many Gaelic placenames, with Gaelic remaining the majority language until the nineteenth century.

ROBERT THE BRUCE

The year 1306 was a tumultuous period for Robert the Bruce, an ambitious nobleman with his eye on the Scottish crown, then held by the English King Edward I, 'Hammer of the Scots'. He stabbed his rival Comyn in front of the altar of Greyfriars Monastery in Dumfries, a major act of sacrilege; he had himself crowned King at Perth in defiance of Edward, and without the full support of other nobles; he fought and lost two battles against the English; he saw his sister, wife and daughter imprisoned; he was on the ropes, and retired to regroup somewhere in the west, possibly the Hebrides and/or Rathlin Island off Ireland. In early 1307 he started his comeback with a small-scale operation on Arran, which then became his launch pad for a landing on the Ayrshire mainland and a new, spectacularly successful, military campaign which culminated in the triumph of Bannockburn in 1314 over the forces of the ineffective Edward II ('The Hammer' having died in 1307).

The few days Bruce spent on the island have generated an extensive body of legend, much resorted to by (mostly Victorian) cheerleaders of romanticised Arran, and subsequently the tourist trade. He is said to have stayed in THE KING'S CAVE, one of the many locations where he supposedly encountered the spider whose persistence in spinning a web inspired him not to give up. He is then said to set up a position in GLEN CLOY from where he took BRODICK CASTLE, from whose tower he spied the signal from the mainland for the landing. Prior to his departure from KINGSCROSS he spent the night near WHITING BAY, another putative location for the lesson in spidery determination. Tradition then has him granting lands on Arran to the Fullartons of Kilmichael in Glen Cloy for services rendered during the campaign.

The only early account is the metrical epic *The Bruce*, written by John Barbour, Archdeacon of Aberdeen, 1316-1395. Barbour was obviously not an eyewitness, but he had talked to some of the participants, and *The Bruce* is our most reliable chronicle, all later works being merely embroidery. With the exception of the departure from a point on the east coast of the island, none of the elements of the legend are mentioned. No King's Cave. No attack on Brodick Castle (an advance party of Bruce's men did surprise and defeat the garrison out in the open, but the castle itself was not taken, and Bruce was not present at the time). The point where the mainland fire was lit cannot be seen from Brodick Castle. And no mention of the grant of land, a tradition only recorded for the first time by Thomas Pennant in 1772. Overt romanticism came courtesy of Sir Walter Scott's 1815 poem *Lord of the Isles*, which was hugely popular at the time (although to my mind is virtually unreadable) and created more Bruce-ery, some of which later came to be regarded as real (see LOCHRANZA for an example of Scott's fictions becoming transformed into popular notions of genuine Scottish history). So, all in all, the Bruce connection is, with a few exceptions – he was on the island for a time, he did leave from there to the Ayrshire coast – most probably flim-flam. For the hitherto unsuspected connection between Robert the Bruce and *Thunderbirds*, see the chapter on ARRAN AND POPULAR CULTURE.

SMUGGLING

Smuggling looms large in the folk history of the island, particularly in relation to the illegal distillation of whisky in the eighteenth century. Mackenzie MacBride in *Arran of the Bens the Glens and the Brave* estimates there were thirty-two illicit stills in 1784 and fifty in 1797. Numerous tales are told of encounters with the excise men (known as gaugers) and other unwelcome arms of the law. Many of these stories are of the 'cunning peasants outwit the dastardly officials' type; others ended in violence and death. Whisky-making fell into decline in the early nineteenth century when the Duke of Hamilton threatened to dispossess any tenant convicted of illegal distillation. Smuggling also involved other goods on which high taxes were placed, such as salt.

FINGAL AND THE FINGALIANS

Fingal (also known as Fhionn and Fion) was a kind of King Arthur figure from Irish mythology. With his war-band the Fingalians (or the Fhianna) he was at the centre of an entire mythos of interrelated stories of heroism, love, magic, treachery and supernatural encounters. The tales travelled to Scotland with Gaelic storytellers who adapted them to the local geography. As a result similar events from the mythology are anchored in many different Scottish locales, Arran being just one of them. Fingal spent time in the KING'S CAVE; his son Ossian was born and died on the south end of the island; and other characters pop up here and there in traditions and placenames, usually where there is a chambered cairn or other monument. In one of the stories a band of Fingalians, represented as giants, tell a Christian holy man (typically St Patrick) tales of their adventures on Arran, the island being the best hunting ground in the world.

SOURCES

Without a doubt the key published source for the material in this book is the two-volume *The Book of Arran*. Volume 1, *Archaeology*, edited by J.A. Balfour, came out in 1910, and Volume 2, *History and Folklore,* edited by W.M. MacKenzie, followed four years later (from hereon they are referred to as *Book of Arran 1* or *Book of Arran 2*). The latter in particular holds a wealth of stories on fairies, witchcraft, folk magic and the supernatural. Both volumes were republished in the 1980s. The most accessible work on the island's archaeology is Horace Fairhurst's splendid *Exploring Arran's Past*, as well as the websites mentioned in the archaeology section above.

In terms of early works, Arran merits a brief mention in Sir Donald Munro's *A Description of the Western Isles of Scotland Called Hybrides,* written in 1549 and first published in 1774. Valuable descriptions are found in the pioneering works of Martin Martin (*A Description of the Western Islands of Scotland circa 1695*), and Thomas Pennant (*A Tour in Scotland*, 1772). In 1768 James Robertson wrote his *Tour through some of the Western Islands, etc.*, although it was not published until the late nineteenth century, and the circumstances of why and for whom the tour was conducted remain unknown. The Revd James Headrick wrote his *View of the Minerology, Agriculture, Manufactures and Fisheries of the Island of Arran* in 1807, a work which is however rife with Presbyterian priggishness. John McArthur's influential *The Antiquities of Arran with a Historical Sketch of the Island* came out in 1861. Subsequent investigation has revealed that McArthur depended a great deal on hearsay, and had not visited many of the monuments he described. As a result his notes should be treated with caution. Extracts from some of these works, along with much more, can be found in Hamish Whyte's very useful 1997 book *An Arran Anthology*. An invaluable 'people's perspective' view can be found in *Isle of Arran Heritage*, published by the Arran Heritage Community Group, in which pupils interviewed elderly members of the island community and recorded their memories and folklore.

All other sources, including newspapers, magazines, websites and unpublished works, are noted in the text, and refer to the full bibliography at the end.

A number of items on mythology, folklore and magic have no specific location other than 'Arran', so I have collected them here as a taster for the geographically-based chapters to follow.

CELTIC MYTHOLOGY

Manannan Mac Lir, the chief Irish sea god, extended his protection to Arran, where he had a palace called Emhain of the Apple Trees. Attempts have been made to derive 'Avalon' from Emhain.

The Book of Invasions, a pseudo-historical epic setting out the mythical origins of the Irish, tells how the god-men of the Tuatha De Danann defeated the Fir Bolg, another magical race then resident in Ireland. The Fir Bolg (pronounced 'Fir Vulag') survivors fled to Islay and Rathlin Island, the Isles of Man and Arran.

CUSTOMS AND FOLK MAGIC

From *The Book of Arran 2:*

If a mother entered a house before her child was baptised it would bring bad luck to the house.

Sleepwalkers had not had enough water applied at baptism. The cure was to throw the water left after a christening in the face.

At the end of the harvest the last stalks were called the cailleach, the old woman (or witch). Someone, usually an old man, was chosen to tie the bunch of stalks together. Then everyone was blindfolded, handed a sickle, and given the chance to cut the cailleach. When it was done there was a celebration and the cailleach would be taken home and hung up in the kitchen until next spring. If a hare, rabbit, rat or mouse jumped out just before the last cutting, the people would shout, 'There's the Cailleach!'

Cures and healing rituals recorded by Allan Paterson Milne in *Arran: An Island's Story*:

Epilepsy – cured by killing a black cock, but only if it was buried either at the spot where the fit first occurred or under the patient's bed.

A sty – rub a cat's tail on the infected eyelid.

A sore knee – fill a bottle with frogspawn and then bury it.

Adder bites – apply a poultice of ash or rowan bark.

Bleeding wounds – cover with a spider's web.

Sore eyes – 1. apply the first spittle of the morning; 2. use a bunch of bishop-leaves to sprinkle a fluid made from the same plant over and across the eyes – it was essential that the patient gaze steadfastly at the setting sun during the procedure.

Thirst – lift a stone, spit below it, carefully replace stone. Also, possibly, impale a snail on a thorn in a hedge.

Headaches – make a paste of water, salt and soot. Take three sips. Dip the middle finger in the mix and make a cross on the forehead and on the back of the head.

Rheumatism – carry a small potato in the pocket. This was both cure and prophylactic. For best results the potato should be stolen.

Sprained joints – rub on the oil made from the liver of a porpoise.

Measles and whooping cough – find in the hills a saucer-shaped stone which held water. Sprinkle yourself with the water and take three sips. It was essential that both stone and ritual were out of sight of the sea.

Tooth extraction – give the tooth to the patient, who must throw it over the left shoulder.

In a 1900 article from the journal *Folklore*, Malcolm MacPhail recorded an apotropaic ritual which took place in Arran in 1810, at the start of the spring ploughing season. At the very place where the ploughing was to begin, the plough and the horses' harness were sprinkled three times with a solution of salted water. A little of the water was then poured into the animals' ears. Only when this ritual was completed could the labour begin.

Francis Thompson, in *The Supernatural Highlands*, says that Easter Sunday in the Hebrides was A' Chaisg, 'the death day of the eggs', as many eggs were rolled down slopes. In Arran the eggs were used for divination, seeking the names of future husbands and wives.

At the festival of Beltane or Beltaine, usually 1 May, there was a fire ritual designed to both protect against evil and promote fertility. All fires were extinguished at sundown and re-kindled from the sacred 'need-fire' which was either kept alight through the night or lit at dawn. This was the time of year when cattle were sent up to the higher slopes for summer grazing, and the herds were driven through the fire for purification. In *Carmina Gadelica* Alexander Carmichael says the last need-fire was lit on Arran in 1820, although 1895 is also given as the last recorded festival.

A passage in 'At The Rising of The Moon', a short piece in the collection *The Silence of Amor / Where the Forest Murmurs* by the Celtic mystic Fiona Macleod (the pen name of William Sharp) has the following:

> I heard a singular fragment of owl-folklore once on the island of Arran. The narrator said the white owl had seven distinct hoots… the seventh was when the 'Reul Fheasgair' ceased to be the Evening Star and became the 'Reul na Maidne,' the Day-Star. Was this a memory of some myth associating the owl with the other world (or darkness or moontide or Night) disclosed every eve at the opening of the Gates of Dusk?

The 'Evening Star' and 'Day (or Morning) Star' here is clearly Venus when it is seen after sunset or before dawn.

The *Book of Arran 2* also listed sights and sounds which acted as death omens for specific families:

The Cooks – a sound like a slash on a piece of furniture.
The Curries, Sillars and Thomsons – the bodach a' chiopainn, a sound as of a tethering pin being driven into the ground.
The Kerrs and MacMillans – the pìobaire sith, the fairy piper, whose music started sweetly enough and ended in a wail.
The MacKelvies – the apparition of a white lady.
The MacKenzies – a sound like a hammering on the wall.

The Riochd nan Daoine, the Dream Signs of the People, are also listed. In dreams, these animals were said to represent certain clans or families:

Mice – the Bannatynes
Pigs or bulls – the Cooks
Plovers – the Curries
Geese – the Fullartons
Hares – the Hamiltons
Sheep – the Kerrs
Sheep dogs – the MacAlisters or MacDonalds
Bloodhounds – the MacGregors
Doves or pigeons – the MacKelvies
Bees – the MacKenzies
Rabbits – the Mackinnons
Asses – the MacLardys
Pigs – the MacMasters
Woodpigeons – the MacMillans

A dun bull – the MacNeils
Cats – the MacNicols or MacNeishes
Rats – the Robertsons
Frogs – the Sillars
Lions – the Stewarts

The Stewart lion is obvious, the Stewart name being royal. Some of the other associations may be distant memories of totemic animals.

FAIRIES AND OTHER SPIRITS

> The belief in fairies and witches, in the mysteries of Deuteroscopia or Second Sight, and in the power of the Evil Eye, still lingers in the minds of the older inhabitants. (John McArthur, *The Antiquities of Arran*)

There are three places called Fairy Dell or Fairy Glen on the island (near LOCHRANZA, WHITING BAY and the road between BRODICK and LAMLASH), although I suspect they received these names from Anglophone visitors or incomers in the late nineteenth century or later. Earlier fairy associations are usually those placenames featuring the Gaelic word 'sith' (pronounced 'shee'). 'Sithean' and 'Sidhean' ('shee-an') or similar variations usually indicate fairy knolls or hills.

Arran has a very particular distinction in that encounters with fairies are not confined to the folklore of Victorian and earlier periods but have been reported in the twentieth century and to the present day. First though, a selection from *The Book of Arran 2*:

> A farmer working at the plough expressed a desire for a bite to eat. A freshly baked bannock appeared. It was so good he wished for the boll of meal from which it was made. The boll duly appeared and he made wonderful bread with it. In return he left a boll of his own at the spot but the fairies thrashed him because it was not of good quality, so he harvested some top-grain, had it milled, and left it for the fairies. As a result he and they were firm friends until he died.

> When corn was dried on a kiln, a portion had to be left for the fairies or harm would result to the owner of the corn.

> A normally active housewife became very dull and sleepy. As her family kept watch one night they saw fairies enter and transform her into a horse, and then use her to pull the cart all night. In the morning a careful search found the harness hidden in the garden.

> A married man fell in love with a fairy. His concerned wife consulted a wise woman. Her advice was to sprinkle oatmeal on her husband's back as he was leaving the house to visit his lover – this caused him to see the fairy as very ugly, so he immediately abandoned her.

> Fairies danced on the circular patches of a tough and hard grass called tasinn air geim, which grew on the moors.

Many years ago a fishing smack crossing from Arran to Ireland started to sink even though there were no leaks. One crewman who possessed the second sight saw a small brown figure on deck. He told another crewman to stand on the top of his feet and look around. This was a standard way for a seer to communicate his vision to another, ungifted person. The second sailor saw that the deck, sailwork and indeed the entire vessel were swarming with brown manikins. The little people explained they were leaving Arran because it was now too holy. Many places in Scotland have a similar tale – the motif of the fairies fleeing from Christianity has a long history, being found in, for example, the 'Wife of Bath's Tale' in Chaucer's *Canterbury Tales* (1380): 'For now the so-great charity and prayers / Of limiters and other holy friars / That do infest each land and every stream / As thick as motes are in a bright sunbeam, / Blessing halls, chambers, kitchens, ladies' bowers / Cities and towns and castles and high towers / Manors and barns and stables, aye and dairies / This causes it that there are now no fairies.'

A brownie in a certain farm was very jealous of any stranger in the house. Once the farmer invited a friend to supper, but the man could not eat because his spoonful of porridge kept slipping back to the plate. The farmer picked up the poker and threw it at a corner, saying 'Get out of this'. All was then well.

A young girl had a handsome sweetheart who would not tell her his name or home. He kept asking her to elope with him, but she just as adamantly refused. Observing that she was always having to work at spinning, he offered to spin a sack of wool for her if she would agree to leave with him. She was grateful for the amount of labour it would save her and so agreed, but added the proviso that she would be free of her promise if she guessed his name before the sack was spun. One night she was crossing a deep stream in a lonely place when she heard a spinning wheel and singing from the bottom of the stream. She saw an old dark wizened man sitting at a large wheel, spinning and singing, 'Oh! Little does my sweetheart know, that 'Crodhanach' is my name.' When he came to her with the completed sack she said 'thank you, Crodhanach' and he disappeared up the chimney in a shower of red sparks. This motif is found in other tales from around the world, such as Tom Tit Tot, Rumpelstiltskin and Whuppity Stoorie.

The Book of Arran also describes entities other than fairies. A bocan or baukan was a 'dreaded visitant from another world'. These malevolent spirits, sometimes called hobgoblins, were usually seen near fords or bridges or at lonely places on the road or on the shore. A bocan could not speak to you unless you spoke to it first, and if asking a question you should always say 'in the name of God'. They were generally known by the name of the person who saw them – Donald's Bocan, Betty's Bocan etc. Sometimes bocans took the form of an animal or a ship. For more on specific bocans, see CLAUCHLANDS, THE STRING, MACHRIE MOOR and WHITING BAY.

In 1936, *John O'London's Weekly*, a literary magazine, published a series of letters from people who claimed to have seen fairies. In the 28 March edition, Struan Robertson wrote:

One afternoon in Arran I saw ten fairies playing out and in among gorse bushes and round about the grazing sheep. The sheep were quite undisturbed except that if a fairy went too near one of them then it would trot off for a few yards. Wandering in a wood in Arran one morning I heard the silvery plangent accents of fairies, and following the sounds I saw quite a clan of them hurrying along a green footpath. They seemed angry about something. Observing me, they chattered loudly, scattered as one sees a flock of excited sparrows scattering, increased their speed and fled.

Robertson had previously met a fairy near Aberfoyle in his native Stirlingshire.

The most recent fairy encounter I have been able to find was in the January 2004 issue of *Fortean Times* (No. 179), which carried an article called 'Invitation to Elfland' by the author Moyra Doorly. In it she described meeting at least eight different kinds of fairies or nature spirits when she lived on Arran – and the dangers attendant in this. For several months she had been, with no clear aim, practicing meditation techniques which involved 'detaching the vision from the object by focusing beyond it and allowing the mind to rest' so that the reality of a given environment revealed itself. Then, out of the blue, on a mild summer evening in a garden by a stream, she saw 'a procession of little figures led by a faun… the faun was small – about 3ft (90cm) tall – and seemed pleased with himself. I saw short legs strutting with pride and heard tiny hooves clip-clopping on the paving stones.' The creature was the classic fairytale faun, with shaggy legs, horns about 6ins (15cm) long and a wrinkled face. Moyra panicked and ran into the house, finding solace in the reality of mundane television news. Then her partner, Peter, saw the faun too, although he couldn't see the other beings clearly. The faun was by the stream and seemed agitated, as if by some kind of male rivalry issue.

Thereafter Moyra and Peter, intoxicated by the first encounter, set out to encourage more visitors. They left oats and milk out, played the bagpipes, a handheld drum and a bodhran, and built a little shrine beside the stream. More shrines were planned at key points around the island, but in the end only three were constructed. Their project worked. An elf dressed in mottled greens and browns, and of the size of a six-year-old boy but with an ancient face, came into the house. On a hot summer afternoon Peter saw little sylph-like beings flying among the flowers. And Moyra was taken by a second procession of beings from the stream into a rock-hewn hall in which a feast had been prepared. Small cheerful imps in bright green tried, unsuccessfully, to get her to put on the clothes they offered. And a different group of taller grey-haired beings, which Moyra dubbed the 'stripies' because of their striped clothes of browns and greens, stood very still, apparently waiting to see if she would sit at their table. The stripies had an unpleasant languorous, narcotic air about them. Then Moyra heard the words: 'You are the first person to come this way for 200 years. Come and be with us.' At this point she turned away and found herself back at the stream, aware that she had just escaped from a dangerous threat. Peter, it turned out, had also been invited to go away. Both had come close to the classic fairy abduction, in which humans willingly entered an underground hall, but found themselves trapped in a place where time proceeded at a slower pace than in the outside world. Worried, they dismantled the shrines and avoided the stream.

Later, walking in the forest, Moyra heard a strange singing and saw small, bright 'fairy lights', 4-6ins (10-15cm) in diameter, which hovered for a time before doing a little dance in the air and shooting off at great speed. In early autumn she encountered another part of the fairy demographic, unfriendly beings which looked like trees stripped of their eaves, which she dubbed the 'stiks'. Several of them stood around her in a hostile manner, one saying: 'Why are you here? This is no place for you.' Later in the year she came across the 'misties', beings of cold dense mist who created a sense of temporary confusion (familiar to those lost in a forest).

The encounters stopped when Moyra left Arran, although she still caught glimpses of nature spirits in a park or a set of potted plants on a friend's city flat. The article includes three further fascinating points. Firstly, a local folklore expert had told Moyra that the fairies left Arran when electricity came, but she concluded that people, beguiled and distracted by the sights, lights and sounds of modern life, simply stopped being able to see them – and to see them you needed to develop a quietist state of mind. Secondly, the best place to encounter fairies may be, paradoxically, in or near recent forestry plantations, which although man made, regular and often deplored as ugly and unnatural, are left untouched after planting, thereby becoming 'set aside' zones which allow nature beings to flourish. And thirdly, be careful what you wish for, if what you wish for is to meet fairies. You may not like what you find.

THE EVIL EYE

The *Book of Arran 2* has numerous examples of the belief in the evil eye – the ability, willed or unconscious, to cause harm or death by a mere glance. Edward Cook, for example, who died a few years before 1914, and lived in the south end of the island, could kill a litter of pigs or a foal with just a look.

One woman so feared that her one cow would have the eye put on it that she always put excess salt in any milk she supplied to someone else. This was an apotropaic ritual, salt being a common prophylactic against evil.

An old lady remembered being told of an older generation who were concerned there was unintended evil in their glance, so they always blessed an animal before looking at it with Gaelic phrases meaning 'That God may bless the beast', or 'May God bless the thing my eye is regarding'. Here *The Book of Arran 2* is quoting from *Evil-Eye in the Western Highlands* by R.C. MacLagan, published in 1902. Other common phrases were 'He put his eye on it' (anything bewitched) and 'I do not heed your eye,' said to divert the evil eye.

A man riding home late passed a man whom he thought he recognised and so spoke briefly to. But before he got home his horse broke out in a frothing sweat. Nothing could be done. A consultation concluded the horse had been cronached, bewitched. Someone with the skill of eòlas a' chronachaidh, the counter charm, was sent for. On his arrival he asked the rider if he had met anyone? Yes. Had he spoken to him? Yes. This was good, for had he not done so it would have been himself who would have suffered, not his horse. A rite was performed – the correspondent could not remember the details – and the horse jumped up and started to eat. It was customary in meeting any person in the dark of night to address him, as it might be the Devil.

A pinch of oatmeal sprinkled in a beehive protected the bees from the evil eye.

WITCHCRAFT AND BLACK MAGIC

Marion Scott, a girl of eighteen, serving a family in Innerkip parish, Renfrewshire, would go out in the morning with a hair-tether, by pulling which, and calling out,

"God send us milk and mickle [much] of it!" she would supply herself with abundance of the produce of her neighbours' cows. She had a great deal of intercourse with the devil, who passed under the name of Serpent, and by whose aid she used to raise windy weather for the destruction of shipping. One day, being out at sea near the island of ARRAN, she caused Colin Campbell's sails to be riven, but was herself overset with the storm, so as to be thrown into a fever. After a night-meeting with Satan, he conveyed her home in the dawning, and when she was come near the house where she was a servant, her master saw a waif of him as he went away from her. (Robert Chalmers, *Domestic Annals of Scotland From the Reformation to the Revolution: Reign of Charles II, 1660-1673*)

Sir Fergus Barclay, the 'De'il of Ardrossan', had a reputation as a sorcerer and a habitué of Satan. He is supposed to have died on Arran and buried on a beach here – in one version of the story, in a shroud made from a bull's hide. However on the night of the burial a great storm disinterred the body and swept it back to Ardrossan, where it was reburied. A stone in Ardrossan church supposedly marks the spot, and the legend has it that to take earth from the grave and throw it into the sea would call up storm and flood.

Once again, *The Book of Arran 2* has a good crop of witchcraft stories. Some concerned the fishing industry – up to 1884, for example, fishermen on a trip would boil pins in a pot to keep away the witches – but most dealt with farming, and specifically, the bewitching of cattle and milk. If a witch could get the name of a cow or a hair from her tail, and also see the milk, she could transfer the cow's milk to her own cow via sympathetic magic. A boot tacket or nail put in the wood at the mouth of a churn would protect it from witchcraft, but sometimes other methods were required.

A particular cow had been bewitched by the wife of a neighbour, so it would not give milk. The farmer's daughter broke the spell by putting an oatmeal bannock about the size of a five-shilling piece in the pail before starting the milking. This took place in the 1860s.

In 1868-69 a young boy went with a woman in her sixties on a covert mission to save a sick cow. The husband disdained superstition, so on the pretence of going gathering herbs she and the boy climbed a hill and kept along the ridge until they came to a deep ravine, in which, in the pines, was the little thatched cottage of the wise woman. She handed over a black quart bottle, muttered some words, and instructed them not to speak to anyone on their way home. To achieve this they took the country route away from the houses. The cure was administered secretly and the cow recovered. The young lad, now a grown man reciting the tale in the 1900s, regarded it as a very vivid memory from his childhood.

When the milk would not produce butter, collective action was required to break the spell. The milk was poured into the churn, which was like a narrow barrel placed on end, and churned with a perforated float the diameter of the churn. This float had a long handle. One person took the churn and worked the float chanting:

McFarlane sought a drink of milk (Fither an ninnty nandy)
He sought a drink and he got none (Fither an ninnty nandy)
Fither an ninnty, ninnty, ninnty, ninnty, ninnty, ninnty.

At the same time the person kept time with the stroke of the churn. Then another took his place with the same chant while the first person went round the churn chanting the same. When the second was finished the third took his place, the second holding hands with the first and chanting the same, and so on until a circle was formed around the churn. This took place up to the 1860s. The McFarlane of the chant, the story went, was passing a farmhouse one day and asked for a drink of milk. Because it was half-churned into butter he was refused, so he put some meal or some other item into the churn as revenge, and the butter would not come.

PROPHECIES

In March 1991 David Icke, under apparent guidance from various higher beings, predicted that Arran would be hit by a huge earthquake before the end of the year and would sink beneath the sea. As far as I can tell, this has not taken place.

UFOS

In 2004 West Kilbride on the Ayrshire mainland had the highest number of recorded sightings of UFOs in Britain – twelve in total. A piece in *The Scotsman* (2 February 2006) noted that many of these were seen in the direction of Arran, sometimes hovering over the water. Helicopters and landowners' private aircraft seemed to be the most likely culprits.

Brodick Castle – detail of a mirror frame in the Old Library.

1

BRODICK

Brodick is the main ferry port, where the vast majority of visitors arrive, and has the preponderance of facilities. Brodick today is on the south part of the bay, but the original village was at Mossend, on the north side, near Cladach.

BRODICK CASTLE★★★

(NS01553786). Owned by the National Trust for Scotland, its opening hours are: castle 30 March to 31 October, daily 11 a.m. to 4.30 p.m. (closes 3.30 p.m. in October); country park: all year, daily 9.30 a.m. to sunset; reception centre, shop and walled garden: 30 March to 3 October, daily 10 a.m. to 4.30 p.m. and 1 November to 21 Dececember Friday/Saturday/Sunday, 10 a.m. to 3.30 p.m. Telephone: 0844 493 2152. Admission charge for the castle.

Brodick Castle is one of the must-see sights of Arran. Both the rooms, with their collections of paintings, furniture, porcelain and other *objets d'art*, and the extensive gardens and country park are full of marvels and wonders, and you should allow at least half a day for a thorough look round.

The castle has been a defensive position probably since Viking times, and in the Middle Ages had a turbulent history of burning, rebuilding and occupation, followed by further cycles of destruction and reconstruction. The royal houses of Bruce and Stuart, the monarchs of Scotland and England, the Hamiltons, the Campbells, the MacLeans, the MacDonald Lords of the Isles, the forces of Oliver Cromwell – they've all fought over this much-disputed fortress on a much-disputed island. What you see these days is basically the work of more settled times – a grand nineteenth-century stately home, albeit one with a medieval core. The interiors and the Victorian Baronial architecture are mostly the legacy of successive dukes of Hamilton, for whom this was a popular hunting lodge and summer dwelling. The first gardens date from the early eighteenth century, and have been developed at successive stages so that they are now a nationally important collection – and a pleasure to stroll around even for those who suffer from terminal horticultural ignorance. The last Hamilton owner was Mary, Duchess of Montrose, daughter of the 12th duke. Since her death in 1957 the castle has been owned by the National Trust for Scotland.

An excellent guidebook is for sale within the castle and there are information boards and knowledgeable volunteer guides in every room, and very detailed information on the country park is available in the visitor centre by the main car park and in the ranger centre. For these reasons I will concentrate here only on the quirky, the curious and the allegedly paranormal.

Brodick Castle, with the oldest parts in the foreground.

Brodick Castle: detail
of the Victorian
crenellations on the west
tower.

Brodick Castle and William Beckford

Beckford's schemes... were as grandiose and ambitious as those of an Eastern caliph. (Edith Birkhead, *The Tale of Terror: A Study of the Gothic Romance*)

[Beckford] was drawn instinctively to anything irregular, odd, exotic or fantastic. (Roy Strong, *Lost Treasures of Britain*)

He actively promoted his own myth, elaborating, or possibly inventing stories about himself. (Ian Dejardin, *William Beckford 1760-1844: An Eye for the Magnificent*)

I shall never be… good for anything in this world, but composing airs, building towers, forming gardens, collecting old Japan, and writing a journey to China or the Moon. (William Beckford to Lady Catherine Hamilton, quoted in James Lees-Milne, *William Beckford*)

William Beckford was a pioneering Gothic novelist, the eighteenth-century equivalent of a billionaire, and one of the most extraordinary collectors and rich eccentrics who ever lived. Brodick Castle is home to the largest collection of Beckfordiana in the world. Items he owned – or items associated with him – are scattered throughout the rooms, and as some of these items are Very Strange Indeed, a little background is in order.

William Beckford was the world's richest gay Goth (if he were alive today, he would doubtless cleave towards the lacier and more velvet end of the Goth sub-culture, probably mooning about listening to the melancholic strains of The Cure). He was an aesthete who combined an exquisitely pleasurable appreciation of the beautiful and odd with an over-riding sense of guilt, doom and self-destruction. He loved nature, seclusion, mystery, shadows, the exotic and anything designed to overwhelm the senses. At the age of sixteen he wrote *Biographical Memoirs of Extraordinary Painters*, a spoof art-historical study of a number of fictional artists with ludicrous names. His short fiction from the same period was written in a voluptuous and exaggerated prose style, the subject matter often being morbid and decadent. The key symbol in these early works is the tower – the strange edifice, home of power, magic and mystery. It was a motif that was to dominate Beckford's work and life.

In 1786, at the age of twenty-five, Beckford wrote *Vathek*, a cod 'Arabian Nights' fantasy-horror novel. The eponymous Caliph, who lords it over his domain from a vast multi-roomed tower, sets off on a quest initiated by the demon Eblis. This journey leads to magical situations and meetings with extraordinary and often unpleasant characters (some of whom are clearly poison portraits of Beckford's despised relatives). The whole episode ends with Vathek filled with self-loathing and tormented by pain in a subterranean Hell. Along with Horace Walpole's *The Castle of Otranto* (1764), The *Mysteries of Udolpho* by Mrs Radcliffe (1794) and *The Monk* by Matthew Gregory Lewis (1795), Vathek was one of the first Gothic novels, a new style of fiction which used horror, fantasy and 'atmosphere' to inculcate a sense of the sublime and terror in the reader. This literary strain later flourished, its highpoints being Mary Shelley's *Frankenstein* and *Dracula* by Bram Stoker, and is now one of the most popular fictional genres. Vathek, despite its awkwardness, its straining for effect and its almost non-existent plot, can still be read with pleasure today:

> To read *Vathek* is like falling asleep in a huge Oriental palace after wandering alone through great, echoing halls resplendent with a gorgeous arras, on which are displayed the adventures of the caliph who built the palaces of the five senses. In our dream the caliph and his courtiers come to life, and we awake dazzled with the memory of a myriad wonders. (Edith Birkhead, *The Tale of Terror*).

Left to his own devices, Beckford would probably have become a kind of precursor of the great horror writer H.P. Lovecraft, churning out clumsily written but strangely compelling fictions which reflected his own unique sensibility. But it was not to be. Sexually ambivalent throughout his life, Beckford was caught up in a homosexual scandal (although there is some doubt he was actually observed *in flagrante* as was implied at the time). Despite his wealth, he found himself completely ostracised from English society. Beckford responded by turning his back on that society. He travelled extensively in Europe. He became an art collector *in excelsis*. And he built Fonthill Abbey, which 'represents perhaps the most fantastic episode in British architectural history. It arose brashly out of the Wiltshire landscape as a huge gesture of revenge against a society which had condemned its creator to social obloquy.' (Roy Strong, *Lost Treasures of Britain*).

> Edifices manifest a principle central to the description of most physical structures in fantasy: there is always more to them than meets the eye. Because of the centripetal force they exert on the mind's eye, edifices tend to dominate their landscape. In a physical sense, this is obvious; but it is also the case that those who rule edifices... tend also to be ruled by them, in the sense that they become tied to – and identified with – their abodes. (John Clute and John Grant, *The Encyclopedia of Fantasy*)

Fonthill Abbey was not a religious structure. It was not the product of piety. It was the product of mania – and of almost inexhaustible wealth. The abbey was the ultimate folly, a gargantuan, never-finished project, a building both magnificent and mad. Everything about it was extraordinary. It was a house that aped the nature and shape of a grand medieval Gothic cathedral, but the proportions were all wrong, one part being excessively long and narrow, others too tall or too short. The dimensions were Herculean. North to south it was 312ft (95m) long, which is the same size as the nave and sanctuary of Westminster Abbey. From west to east it measured 270ft (82m). The two octagonal turrets on the east transept were 120ft (36.5m) high. At 276ft (84m) high the central tower, one of the tallest structures in England, dominated the landscape for miles around. If the intended spire had been built it would have been the single tallest building in Europe – the ultimate middle-finger kiss-off to the world Beckford despised. Doors were deliberately over-sized to distort perspective. The central space under the tower was left open so that your gaze went up... and up. The interior décor made use of lighting effects, curtains and shadows to accentuate the sense of gloom and mystery. The grounds were surrounded by a wall 12ft (3.6m) high and 7 miles (11.2km) long (which enraged the local squirearchy because it prevented fox-hunting, a sport Beckford loathed). A million trees were planted. The landscape was manipulated so that the route of the entrance drive between the trees allowed the abbey to loom into view with maximum impact. Artists flocked to see Fonthill. Constable called it 'a romantic place, quite fairy land.' Turner was haunted by the tower, painting it several times in different weather conditions. At times the abbey could seem ethereal; in bad weather it seemed positively sinister. As Nikolaus Pevsner has written, Fonthill Abbey was designed 'to create sentiments of amazement, of shock, even of awe... [it was] the most prodigious romantic folly in England.'

And within, Beckford, with a few servants, friends and catamites, enjoyed his cabinet of curiosities. He dined on exquisite porcelain, each set consisting of non-matching items, and each set used for only one day a year. He took enjoyment in art, furniture, precious stones, silverware, old books, goldware, statues and chinaware. And he became something of a Howard Hughes figure *avant la lettre*, a rich, largely solitary eccentric inhabiting a museum-like edifice not unlike *Citizen Kane*'s Xanadu, his isolation and sense of gloom accentuated by the early death of his beloved wife. He planned his mausoleum, a 'Revelation Chamber' with a coffin placed on a jasper floor and view-able to 'pilgrims' through a wire chamber. And once, just once, he held a social event. In 1800 Lord Nelson, the hero of the hour, dined at the abbey. He was accompanied by Lady Hamilton, an old friend of Beckford from Italy, and hence able to overcome the social exclusion zone the British nobility had placed on Beckford. The couple's route was lined with rows of silent hooded figures holding lighted torches, a typically theatrical spectacle from a host who delighted in artifice and atmosphere.

Sadly, Fonthill Abbey is no longer to be seen. Beckford's fortune declined and in 1822 he was forced to sell up. Shortly afterwards the vast central tower collapsed. The damage was too great to repair and after standing as an awe-inspiring ruin for a while the site was quarried for building stone. Beckford moved to Bath, where, still obsessed with towers, he built and lived in the slightly more modest 154ft (47m) high Lansdown Tower. The top of the tower is a replica of the Lysicrates Monument in Athens, a favourite theme for folly builders. The house now functions as a mortuary chapel, and can be visited. Beckford himself is buried in the adjacent cemetery.

Beckford's treasures were dispersed both during and after his lifetime. Brodick Castle holds the world's largest collection of Beckfordiana, courtesy of the fact that his youngest daughter, Susan Euphemia, married the 10th Duke of Hamilton. Look for items decorated with Beckford's family crest, a heron with a fish in its beak (a visual pun from the phrase *bec fort*, French for 'strong bill'). More of his furniture and ceramics can be seen at another National Trust property, Charlecote Park, near Stratford-on-Avon.

If you want to find out more about the amazing William Beckford and Fonthill Abbey, the best books are Boyd Alexander's *England's Wealthiest Son: A Study of William Beckford*; *Lost Treasures of Britain* by Roy Strong; Brian Fothergill's *Beckford of Fonthill*; and *William Beckford* by James Lees-Milne.

Brodick Castle – Ghosts
The castle has a persistent tradition of several ghosts, whose supposed activities have been widely disseminated through websites and books. The original sources for most of the stories of paranormal activities are the autobiographical writings of Lady Jean Fforde, such as *Castles in the Air*, published in 1982, and a piece in *Tales from Scottish Lairds* (1985). Lady Jean is the daughter of Mary, the Duchess of Montrose, the cas-tle's last aristocratic inhabitant, who died in 1957, after which the National Trust for Scotland took ownership. Lady Jean identified three main spirits:

1. A man dressed in a green velvet coat and light-coloured breeches, seen reading in the library.

2. A white deer seen on the hill when the head of the resident family dies. A silver-grey hind was seen just before Lady Jean's father, the duke, died. 'A pure white calf was born four months after my mother died and another born before my brother, Lord Ronald, died.' White deer are uncommon but not unknown, and the description makes it clear these are flesh and blood animals, not spirits. The association between the deer and the deaths seems tenuous, and is I suggest a holdover from a time when white deer attracted awe and reverence.

3. The 'Grey Lady'. Initially this was a ghost with which children in the castle were threatened, in the time-honoured tradition of 'Go to bed or the Grey Lady will catch you'. Then when the duchess became ill in the late 1950s the Grey Lady started to be seen in the back quarters of the house. Although the core story is in *Castles in the Air*, more detail can be found in Peter Underwood's book *This Haunted Isle*. In 1984 the property controller, John M. Forgie, told Underwood that neither he nor his family had seen the Grey Lady in ten years of residence, but that Lady Jean Fforde's son was supposed to have seen her when he was child. Lady Jean wrote to Underwood that the 1950s ghost was seen from different viewpoints and usually described as looking like a dairymaid. She was most often seen going down a back stairway, or followed into the servants' hall, where she always disappeared. One morning the butler noticed her walk down the stairway and appear to talk to an odd-job man who was scrubbing the floor in the passage. The man later denied that anyone had spoken to him.

The accumulated descriptions suggest the Grey Lady was seen by at least four people, including two grooms, a man named Watson, and the housekeeper, Mrs Munsey. Mrs Munsey believed in automatic writing and as a result was badgered by the staff and some of the family into trying to communicate with the ghost. Automatic writing is used by some mediums – they encourage a disembodied spirit to use their body as a 'channel' with which to write. It has been much criticised as basically being the medium's subconscious at work, and is notorious for claims of giants of literature and music returning from the dead to allegedly pen new 'masterpieces'. Through the controlled writing Mrs Munsey learned that the ghost had been in the household when Cromwell's garrison was stationed there, and conceived a baby by one of the officers. She was turned out of the castle and disowned by her family, so she committed suicide at the Old Quay below the castle.

Castles in the Air also mentions that during renovations in the back quarters, a wall which sounded hollow if tapped was opened up, and a heap of rubble fell out. Willie Davidson, who farmed Glen Rosa, told the duchess a (possibly apocryphal) story of three women who had died from the plague. Their bodies had been thrown down a secret passage leading to the shore, and covered with quicklime and rubble. This was supposed to have taken place in 1700. 'When we got home my mother instructed the builders to replace the rubble and plaster up the hole and make no further excavations in case any germs would escape!' *Castles in the Air* does not link the plague story with the Grey Lady, but this has not stopped several others suggesting this as an alternative origin for the ghost. So we have the pregnancy-suicide origin theory derived from the dubious method of automatic writing, and the plague-death origin theory which is not mentioned in the primary source but has been conflated later. If the Grey Lady does wander the corridors and stairs, she may well be unrelated to either. Bill Caswell, the current custodian, has seen nothing in nine years' residence, but twice his cat, coming in through the back door, stopped at the bottom of stairs, stared at a cupboard, arched its back, and spat, even though nothing was visible.

In July 2003 the organisation SPI (Scottish Paranormal Investigations) undertook a ghost hunt at the castle (see www.scottishparanormalinvestigations.co.uk). The group included mediums who identified several spirits, although of course none of these can be objectively verified. The investigation was largely inconclusive – the key findings, if such they are, are mentioned in the paragraphs on the relevant rooms.

Brodick Castle – Exterior
The *Ayr Observer* of 4 June 1844 reported on the start of the rebuilding of the castle, a wedding present from the Duke of Hamilton for his son the Marquis of Douglas and Clydesdale and his bride Princess Marie of Baden. The foundation stone was laid with Masonic honours accompanied by a prayer and the pouring of corn, wine and oil on the stone – the usual Masonic emblem of plenty. A foundation deposit was placed in the stone, consisting of a sealed bottle containing all the coins of Queen Victoria, an *Edinburgh Almanack* of 1844, a newspaper of the day, and a variety of other articles provided by the marquis and the princess. The older, eastern part of the castle can be identified by finding the clearly visible join on the main south front – the clue is the difference in size of the windows on the first floor. The low wall further to the east was erected by Cromwell's troops in 1652 as a battery for cannon. A great tower was constructed on the old wall as part of the rebuilding, but within a few months was toppled by a great storm. There is a persistent tradition of a secret tunnel linking the castle to the shoreline, although a geophysical survey in 2001 found only a nineteenth-century drain to the west of the castle.

Brodick Castle – Interior
The castle has ninety-five rooms, although only the main ones are open to the public. This section follows the standard route around the castle, and as well as pointing out Beckfordiana and locations of alleged paranormal occurrences, also describes the stranger ornamentation and decoration, some of which is easy to miss. Each of the main rooms has a small figure known as a Bogle hidden somewhere – searching for them can provide an absorbing occupation for children. 'Bogle' is a common Scottish word for a spirit or ghostly entity.

Brodick Castle – The Entrance Hall
As if eighty-seven mounted stags' heads wasn't enough, the carved wooden surround of the fireplace has a bearded man with hair made of grapes and vines; four foliate lions' heads; two sets of paired foliate winged lions; and two sets of twinned dolphins or sea monsters. The wooden display double bench opposite boasts two lions as supporters, and a pair of winged souls.

Brodick Castle – The Staircase Landing
The landing is rich in Beckfordiana and repays careful study. The most obvious items are the paintings of Beckford's daughter Susan Euphemia Beckford, and the 1844 death portrait of William Beckford by Willes Maddox★. The latter is a deceptively simple painting – it omits, for example, the Aladdin's Cave clutter of Beckford's bedroom, which was choc-a-bloc with paintings and fine furniture. And is it me or do the vertical and horizontal edges of the curtains appear to form a cross above the corpse? Note that the actual ebony cabinet decorated with a double eagle that can be seen in the deathbed scene stands directly below the painting.

Also displayed on the wall is 'The Temptation of St Anthony' by David Teniers★. It was owned by Beckford. The subject was a popular one for artists as it allowed them to legitimately paint demons in a respectable context. The small painting is itself in a frame which is alive with creatures. The cabinet contains a collection of Beckfordiana carved from semi-precious stones, as well as porcelain, with one piece featuring the head of a heron with a fish in its beak ('*bec fort*'). The four extraordinary Venetian 'blackamoor' stools★ come from the gallery of Fonthill Abbey. The bowed wooden chair★ is decorated with a winged soul, two sea monsters spewing foliage, and a crowned man and woman each with double fish tails. The grandfather clock★ has an image of Europa sitting on the bull. You may find that the face of the sun on the clock reminds you of the conventional representations of Jesus, possibly another pun (sun = the Son).

Brodick Castle – The Private Apartments: The Bathroom, Dressing Room and Bedroom

The tiny entrance hall has several humorous engravings including one of two society ladies with elaborate feather headdresses being chased by angry ostriches. Above the bed in the dressing room is a painting of the family mausoleum in Hamilton, South Lanarkshire. The 10th duke was buried here inside an Egyptian sarcophagus. In the bedroom two of the SPI mediums felt that they were being watched from the corner of the room near the hidden servant's door. Presumably it is in the bedroom that Lady Penelope and Parker find the clue in *The Isle of Arran Mystery* (see the chapter on ARRAN AND POPULAR CULTURE).

Brodick Castle – The Boudoir

Here you can find one of Turner's watercolours of Fonthill Abbey★, as well as a pair of silver gilt light sconces from Fonthill. The tiles around the fireplace are decorated with Biblical scenes and miracles. The carved wooden surround features small bearded men with the bodies and wings of birds, plus two birds in radiance. Bill Caswell, the castle custodian, told me an experience related to him by one of the volunteer guides. A visitor asked the guide in another room who was the man sitting in front of the fire in the Boudoir. The guide replied that no one could have been seated on the furniture as it wasn't allowed. The female visitor became very upset at this, and left. In 2003 the SPI team picked up strong vibrations of someone in the chair to the left of the fireplace. An overnight vigil was held in the room but no phenomena were apparent.

Brodick Castle – The Red Gallery

The archaeology cupboard★ has several items of interest: a model of an urn found in a chambered cairn at CLACHAIG; a collection of flints and pitchstones from TORMORE; several barbed and leaf-shaped arrow heads; an iron bar found in a stone grave at CATACOL farm by John Robertson on 15 April 1936; two bronze axeheads dug up in 1890; and an awl made from narwhal bone found in Church Cave (aka the PREACHING CAVE).

The volunteer guides in the castle maintain a visitor comments book. Most of the entries are relatively mundane, but occasionally something curious is recorded. An entry for 5 August 2005 reads: 'At lunchtime two visitors stopped me in Red Gallery. They felt the presence of a young girl on one of the footmen's chairs and wanted to know what we knew of sightings in that area. They felt that the chairs had been in another house (which they have).' A visitor on the 31st of the same month reported a sensation of cold in the Red Gallery, the Boudoir and the Duke's Bedroom, while the drawing room and dining room were very cold, and the kitchen 'ice cold'. The comment continued: 'felt a presence – feeling within his body.' Another visitor reported seeing a chair move in the Red Gallery. During the 2003 investigation by the SPI one of the team sensed a man standing at the door to the library. He was sporting a tall stovepipe-style hat and was 'between thirty-forty years old, slim build, dark hair and wearing dark knee length trousers and a tailcoat.' The same team member picked up the impression of a little girl running up and down the gallery. A shadow was also seen moving from left to right, between the doors to the library and drawing room. A half-degree drop in temperature was recorded at the time.

Brodick Castle – The Drawing Room
The elaborate heraldic ceiling includes several scenes of miniature St Georges killing equally diminutive dragons. The ornate frames of the mirrors deserve attention – that opposite the entrance contains wyverns★, while the one to the right incorporates the head of a Green Man★. The pair of paintings by Watteau on either side of the mirror – 'The Enchanter' and 'The Enchantress' – belonged to Beckford, as did several of the other smaller pictures. The table★ to the left of the door has monsters galore – wyverns, sea monsters, gryphons and long-necked dragons, as well as four female heads spewing foliage. During the SPI vigil in the Boudoir, banging noises were heard coming from the unoccupied drawing room.

Brodick Castle – The Old Library
Up to now you have been in the nineteenth-century castle; from here on you are moving further back in time – this room is seventeenth century, dating from the Cromwellian period. The two wall cases contain some of Beckford's porcelain collection. Or rather, part of his 'Cabinet of Curiosities'. The left-hand case has such items as a gold bowl with a grotesque face on the front and, on the top, a lion with ruby eyes and movable tongue★; a jug★ supported on some kind of quadruped whose head has been bizarrely twisted through 180 degrees; and two Chinese (?) dogs decorated with metal snakes, snails and small monster heads★. Pride of place, however, must go to the bezoar stone★★.

In the Middle Ages, bezoars were highly prized as a magical antidote to all poisons, and were worth far more than gold. The usual practice was to drink water in which the bezoar had been dipped. Bezoars are items that build up in and obstruct the gut: in animals they are typically stones, while human bezoars can include undigested food, unabsorbed drugs, or unconventional items that have been swallowed. It is clear that Beckford was interested in the magical realm, but it was probably as part of his passion for all things unusual or exotic, and there is no evidence he was ever a practitioner of magic. He may have been aware of a famous if cruel experiment to test the efficacy of a bezoar stone from 1575. A cook was caught stealing silver cutlery. A surgeon called Ambroise Paré – a sceptic regarding the popularly-believed powers of a bezoar – proposed the thief voluntarily take poison; if the bezoar cured him, he could go free. The cook swallowed the poison, applied the bezoar – and spent several days dying in agony. For such a powerful magical object, the Brodick bezoar itself is visually unimpressive, something that Beckford must have felt as well, as he had in encased in a gold filigree holder. Bezoars turn up in modern works such as *Harry Potter and Philosopher's Stone*, where Professor Snape discusses a bezoar during a potions lesson

– 'a stone taken from the stomach of a goat, which will protect from most poisons.' In *Harry Potter and the Half-Blood Prince*, Harry uses a bezoar to save Ron Weasley's life after his friend has accidentally drunk poisoned mead. Volume III (*Dream Country*) of Neil Gaiman's sublime supernatural graphic novel *The Sandman* features a trichobezoar, a bezoar made of hair, 'cut out of a young woman's stomach'.

The second cabinet contains several netsuke★ – demons, a skull with a frog, ogres, a skeleton astride a fish – a Lilliputian pair of fully-working miniature pistols★, a nautilus shell supported by a sea monster★, and other items of beauty or curiosity. The elaborate Venetian frame of the small mirror above the fireplace has a roaring foliate head and mysterious foliate creature★★.

Clare Raymond, one of the previous property managers, thought she saw a man in a chair next to the fire in the library. As she approached he disappeared. This sighting is very similar to the report in Lady Jean Ffordes' *Castles in the Air*, which describes a 1950s sighting, or series of sightings, of a man sitting in a chair beside the fireplace. He is said to be bewigged and to be dressed in a green velvet coat and light-coloured breeches. During the SPI investigation one of the team felt drawn to the fireplace, but when standing next to it he felt his mood swing from normal to morose. The SPI also held a séance here. The mediums picked up two spirits, one a woman called Lynn who was wearing a red dress and was in trouble for swimming in an outdoor pool, and the other a large bearded man who was angry with someone. The report claims: 'After analysing the video footage of the séance, it appears that we have caught small pulses of light,' which were coming from one of the female mediums.

Brodick Castle – The Dining Room
This room, part of the sixteenth-century structure, contains some of the most fascinating pieces in the castle. On the table are two striking eighteenth century figures, the Necromancer★★ and the Fish-seller★. The former, far from being a black magician intending to raise the dead, as the name 'Necromancer' implies, is actually an astrologer, covered as he is with symbols of the Zodiac and holding a telescope and orrery. His companion is equally outlandishly attired, being adorned with the piscine products of his trade. Also on the table is a you-couldn't-make-it-up item, a cigar lighter carved from an ibex horn into the simulacrum of a crocodile★★. Then there are two eighteenth-century porcelain tureens in the shape of geese★ – one has an eel in its mouth, the other holds a fish – and several zoomorphic decanters★ in the form of a fish, a seal and a walrus… and a dodo.

Brodick Castle – The Butler's Pantry / The China Room
Cabinets full of china may not be everyone's cup of tea, but look closely and you'll find several strange and curious items:

Item seven: Moustier armorial plates, mid-eighteenth century: plate one, a gryphon being hunted by a costumed horn-blowing monkey on a four-legged monster; plate two, two long-snouted monsters, and a horse-like creature sprouting a pair of horns; plate three, a winged four-legged gryphon, and a horn-blowing humanoid figure bearing wings, a feathery tail and the head of a bird; plate four, a cloaked fox blowing a horn; two monstrous birds squaring off for a fight; and a Red Indian with a bow and arrow and accompanied by a hunting dog.

Item twenty-one: A sixteenth-century Limoges enamel vase and cover by Pierre

Raymond, owned by William Beckford. The decoration includes Classical cherubs, the god Pan, grotesque heads, and birds and monsters.

Items twenty and twenty-two: Four bonbonierres in the shape of pugs' heads. Truly strange. And ugly.

Item twenty-six: Bonbonierres in the shape of a boar's head and pug's head.

Item twenty-seven: A stirrup cup in the shape of a fox's head. It can be stated with certainty that this was not owned by the field-sports-loathing Beckford.

Item twenty-three: Another stirrup cup, this time shaped as the head of a hare.

Brodick Castle – The Bruce Room
A stair leads to the so-called 'Bruce Room', one of the oldest parts of the castle. The name derives solely from the unsubstantiated and unlikely tradition that Bruce stayed in the castle; whereas once it was a major part of the visitor experience, these days, with the tradition undermined by historical scepticism, it is greatly underplayed.

Brodick Castle – The Silver Collection
This is ostensibly a collection of fine objects, here kept in a bank vault-like secure room. Many were owned by Beckford. As with the porcelain, a keen inspection reveals some real oddities.

Item sixty-four: A tea kettle with a spout in the form of a beast.

Item fifty-one: Altar candlesticks decorated with winged souls.

Item fifty-two: A tankard resting on the heads of winged and crested monsters.

Item forty-five: A standing cup and cover. Decorated with a figure who might be Athene, holding a spear and a shield bearing a lion encircled by petals.

Item forty-nine: A late seventeenth-century tureen and cover. The handles are water creatures, the supports are eagles.

Item thirty-one: A nef in the form of a single-masted sailing ship on wheels, with a spout in the shape of a bird's head.

Item fourteen: A wine flagon made from ibis horn.

Item eighteen: A sixteenth-century German flask in the shape of a pig.

Item nine: A family of ten stylised owls**. Made in London in 1877 to Beckford's original designs. Very spooky.

Brodick Castle – The Tea Room and Corridor
Examine the elaborate doll's house in the corridor to find the skeleton in the bedroom. The Tea Room was formerly the servants' hall. Mediumistic investigation by the SPI team reported four spirits in the area: a proud-spirited housekeeper in her late forties or early fifties; an elderly woman who had died no more than twenty-five years ago (this was in 2003); a pale, tall and slim man in his twenties who gave the name George and the date 1820; and an elegant woman in her fifties, who implied that she built the castle, and gave a name that sounded like Edwina Betford (Euphemia Beckford?). The spirit of a black-and-white spaniel was also picked up. Mary, the last duchess, did indeed have such a dog, which is interesting. However, the colour and breed of the dog are both mentioned in the castle guidebook, and this may have influenced the impression. A different member of the team had what could be interpreted as premonitory dreams about the Tea Room before arriving on the island – he could describe its exact layout and the route from the room through the corridor to

Brodick Castle: pine-cone decoration in the Bavarian summer house.

the gents' toilets. In his dream the toilet door opened to reveal a young woman in a 'Victorian servant's' dress. The girl stretched out her arm towards him – but at this point he woke up. Some of the original 1950s sightings of the Grey Lady took place in this corridor.

Brodick Castle – Gardens and Country Park

The formal gardens were started in the early eighteenth century, and extensively developed following the aggrandisement of the old castle into a baronial stately home in 1844, with further improvements made by several generations of passionate aristocratic gardeners. There are numerous paths and routes for walks short and long – if you want to know where you are going, it is best to pick up a map. Or you could just wander serendipitously. Items of interest include the ice house – turn on the light and look down into a very deep and dungeon-like hole where ice was stored for the summer – and the Bavarian summer house, a real oddity, one of four built in 1845 for Princess Marie to remind her of her German homeland. This, the only survivor, was restored in the 1960s. The exterior imitates tree roots, while inside the surfaces are lined with patterns of pine cones. It has a fairytale quality about it, but bearing in mind that fairytales are not always all sweetness and light, it can appear slightly sinister at twilight or in fog. The walled flower garden has the date 1710 carved on the door lintel. A pond in the bog garden is home to a 'cobra lily' carnivorous pitcher plant. Other walks pass the Duchess' Bathing Pool (remember the séance in the library, which picked up a woman who was in trouble for swimming in an outdoor pool?), and the walled Hamilton cemetery, which contains the graves of the 11th duke and the 12th duke and his wife.

For me the most enjoyable path is Dan's Walk, not only because of the lovely woodland, the miniature caves and the fantastic shapes carved into the rock by the Merkland Burn, but also because the trail is scattered with inspirational sculptures★ by Tim Pomeroy of Lamlash. A skein of branches is shaped into the capillaries of a decayed leaf. A stone is carved with a 'canticle' (a song or poem, especially religious in character) of the names of the plants in the woodland – Small Seraphim, Bloody Brittlegill, Lesser Lutestring and Enchanter's Nightshade being but a few. Droplets of 'golden rain' are there to show that although rain is a curse for the tourist, it is a blessing for the natural world (this had the desired reflective effect on me, as I had just been swearing about yet another cloudburst). And two 'croziers' reference both the uncurling of ferns (representing new life) and bishops' staffs (representing spirituality). During the hurricane of 8 January 2008, which brought down many trees across the island, two large conifers fell just inches away from this pair of ammonite-like structures. There is also a footbridge whose railings are made from twisted branches, and which could easily come from a fairytale movie. A loop from Dan's Walk takes you through the heronry. Despite an old legend which states that when the herons departed the dukes of Hamilton would leave the castle, the dukes are gone while the herons remain. The ranger service based in the countryside visitor centre can give advice on walks on the massive estate, including the route up to Goatfell.

Bill Caswell told me that one day, possibly in 2005, the Revd Dr Ian MacLeod and his wife Agnes, walking on one of the country park trails, saw a hooded figure which looked like the subject of Edvard Munch's painting 'The Scream'. It was floating over

Brodick Castle grounds. Dan's Walk – Tim Pomeroy's 'croziers', with the fallen trees that almost hit them.

Brodick – dinosaur on the beach, Cladach.

Pair of standing stones, Deer Park, Brodick.

the ground. They followed it but soon after it disappeared. The Revd MacLeod was minister at Brodick church until he retired in 2006, when he left the island.

BRODICK VILLAGE

The rest of this chapter moves south from Brodick Castle through Brodick itself. Probably the most unexpected sight on Arran is a full-scale model of a dinosaur. The oddly-stanced Tyrannosaurus Rex (or is it an Allosaurus?), a legacy of an art project from the 1970s, is on the shore behind the stained glass and woodworking workshops south of the castle entrance. The easiest way to see the monster is as follows: opposite the entrance to the car park for the Wine Port Restaurant and the brewery at Cladach, and next to the bus shelter, there are two car parking areas. From the left area (the northernmost) a signposted wheelchair-friendly path passes over a new wooden bridge to the sandy beach. From here you get an excellent view of the concrete carnivore to the left (north), across the burn.

The exit drive from the castle to the bridge over the Rosa passes three excellent standing stones* in the area known as the Old Deer Park. A pair respectively 7.5ft (2.3m) and almost 12ft (3.6m) high are easily visible in the field to the west of the road (NS00613744) and a single 8ft (2.5m) high single stone stands east of the drive (NS00723743). They're difficult to see if you are driving but a quick stop will reveal excellent views through the respective field gates. In 1980 ploughing revealed a small cist east of the two stones

One of the many prehistoric cup-and-rings at Stronach.

(NS00643743). The grave was excavated, and re-erected in the ARRAN HERITAGE MUSEUM. The cist and the two standing stones were all in a line, and each about 100ft (30m) apart; the suggestion is that this may be a linear cemetery or some other prehistoric linear feature. Horace Fairhurst (*Exploring Arran's Past*) says that more human remains have been found in the same field as the cist, and, noting the cluster of other prehistoric sites just south of the Rosa Burn, suggests this area was of significant ritual significance. A few metres along the B880 String Road at N00363685 is old Brodick Cemetery, a pleasant if sunless site with lichened late nineteenth-century gravestones.

STRONACH PREHISTORIC ROCK ART★★

Arran has very little prehistoric rock art. But the site at Stronach makes up for that, because it is superb. Take the String Road (B880) and after 400m follow a forestry track (no cars) which leaves the road at NS001367. Walk past the barrier and follow the winding track uphill. After the track has degenerated into a muddy path it comes to the amazing site – a sheet of bedrock carved with large cups, rings and channels. The purpose of these enigmatic marks remains undetermined – current theories take in everything from agricultural, astronomical or ritual functions, to maps, mundane calculations, tribal markings, star charts, identifying totems, or communication with the dead or the gods. If you are so inclined you may see some of the 'tailed' cup-and-ring marks as representing magic mushrooms, haloed beings, or tadpoles.

ISLE OF ARRAN HERITAGE MUSEUM★★

This splendid little museum occupies several former working buildings of various purposes and has a major focus on social, domestic and agricultural history, from a smiddy (blacksmith) to a schoolroom. The café is also highly recommended. If you are researching family or local history the documents archive, open to the public every Wednesday, is an invaluable resource. The museum has its own guide leaflet and the displays are well labelled, so here I will merely point out the items of especial interest.

Archaeology
The reconstructed Bronze Age burial cist, found on the Old Deer Park of the castle in 1980 (see above).
A replica Neolithic skull from KILMORY.
A reconstruction of the face of 'Clachaig Man', created from one of the skulls found in CLACHAIG Chambered Cairn★. Playing beside it is a video of the artist Marvin Elliot reconstructing the prehistoric face. Marvin also carved the various sculptures that dot around CORRIE.
A small cupmarked stone, in two parts, found falling out of the embankment of the Iron Age fort at DRUMADOON. The context suggests the Bronze Age stone was re-used as simple building material by a later culture. It is one of the very few pieces of prehistoric rock art on the island.
Prehistoric axe heads, and arrowheads of flint and pitchstone, found during tree planting and donated by a forestry worker. John McArthur in *The Antiquities of Arran* says that in the Middle Ages this kind of polished stone axe head was called the Purgatory

Hammer, and was thought to be used by the dead to clang at the gates of Purgatory, hoping to be admitted to Heaven.

A Neolithic carved stone ball★, found at DIPPIN in 1891. Several hundred of these artefacts have been found across Scotland, but their function remains a mystery. They were clearly important – great effort was required to carve them – but for what were they used? Suggestions include symbols of rank, such as a chief or priest, or even 'talking stones' – holding the stone in your hand gives you permission to speak up at a tribal gathering or address the gods.

Geology and Paleontology

If you're venturing onto the north-east coastal path be sure to study the photographs of the fossil tracks, the original of which can be seen between SANNOX and LOCHRANZA. The Carboniferous Age creature captured in time was a Myriapod known as Arthropleura or Dipchlinites cuithensis, a kind of cross between a millipede and a centipede, but on a gigantic scale, being at least 3.25ft (1m) long; its twenty-six pairs of appendages were each 4ins (10cm) in length, so just each leg was the size of a good-sized modern Myriapod. A model of the beast can be seen in the Hunterian Museum, Glasgow.

A cast of the fossil footprint of a large reptile called Chirotherium, from the Lower Triassic Age (220-208 million years ago). The track was found on the west coast between the King's Cave and Drumadoon hillfort.

Pitchstone from a sill near CLAUCHLANDS. The hard, glassy rock was frequently used for Neolithic arrowheads and tools.

A real curiosity – a fulgarite★ or fossil lightning strike. Fulgarites (from the Latin for thunderbolts) occur when lightning hits sand, creating a temperature of 1,800°C which fuses the sand into a glassy material. The specimen on show, found near Corrie in 1966, is thought to be the first fulgarite ever identified. To be honest, the small curly hollow tube on display is visually underwhelming, but it's amazing to think that it preserves the effect of a lightning strike 250 million years ago.

A short distance south of the museum a substantial 7ft 10ins (2.4m) high standing stone sits on the east side of the road (NS01003660). In *The Queen's Scotland: Argyll and Bute* Nigel Tranter calls it the Stronach or giant hero's pillar. Bussell (*Arran: Behind the Scenes*) says it is known as the Druid's Stone. Unfortunately its location right next to a busy road – not to mention the encroaching graffiti – has rather robbed it of its grandeur. A fallen standing stone is hidden in the slope of the woods opposite (NS00863652). A little further south a glacial erratic boulder dominates the entrance to the high school (NS003368). Somewhere in the area Thomas Pennant describes 'MacBhrolchin's Stone', a 12ft (3.6m) long recumbent slab: 'It has at one end a crude attempt to carve a head and shoulders. The natives say that it was placed over a giant.' This stone cannot now be found.

GLEN CLOY

Martin Martin (*A Description of the Western Islands of Scotland circa 1695*) recorded the tallest standing stone on Arran as a 15ft (4.5m) monolith on the south side of the Kirkmichael river (as it happens, AUCHENCAR is a little taller). At the foot of this nevertheless huge stone was a cist filled with human bones. Kirkmichael river is now

Left: Statue of Hercules with lionskin shawl, Kilmichael Hotel, Glen Cloy.

Below: Ruined cottage, Glenrickard, Glen Cloy. Site of an alleged 'time slip' experience.

known as the Glencloy Water. Neither menhir nor cist are still with us, and were either lost to the shifting bed of the burn or destroyed for agricultural convenience.

In September 2007 Carol Primrose wrote to me the following:

> Some time in the sixties or early seventies (I can't remember exactly when), my husband and I stayed in the Kilmichael Hotel... The Hotel had an upstairs lounge where residents were served supper of tea and cakes etc. One of the students working there had the job of checking the room was empty then putting out the lights. One day we found her, rather hysterical, giving notice. Several nights running, apparently, she had put the lights out as usual, then found them switched on first thing in the morning. Nobody would admit to doing so and she was so unnerved she wouldn't stay.

As another example of the Cosmic Joker at work, the Fullerton family crest, which sits above the hotel door, contains the motto *Lux in Tenebris* – 'light in darkness'. The hotel grounds contain a number of interesting statues, including Hercules with his lion-skin cloak-trophy. There are also several tree ferns, plants with a long pedigree – they date back to the Carboniferous Era, about 354 to 290 million years ago – which are more usually found in New Zealand and Australia.

Carol also related to me a story told to her by another visitor to the Kilmichael Hotel:

> He claimed that on several occasions he had gone up to the cottage beside the Glenrickard chambered cairn and [seen] a little white dog come out of the door, run across to the cairn to cock its leg, then into the forest beyond. As soon as it appeared a complete stillness fell, no birdsong, no sound of insects or rustling of leaves. Then an old lady appeared at the cottage door and seemed to call the dog which ran back and the two of them went into the house. As soon as they disappeared the birds started to sing. Since the cottage was roofless and ruined we can only assume the old lady and the dog were both ghosts. I have been to the site myself a few times but no ghosts materialised.

The description is of a classic 'time slip' experience rather than of a haunting, although Carol Carol also notes: 'Whether the man who told the story believed it or was pulling our legs I don't know.'

The ruined cottage is still there, slowly decaying in a lonely spot. Glenrickard Chambered Cairn (NS00513466), however, eluded me. A 1977 report on the RCAHMS 'Canmore' website states that a pair of portal stones 2ft and 2ft 9ins (61 and 84cm) high flanked a large chamber, with a second chamber, possibly a secondary insertion, to the north. Either the vegetation has swamped the site since, or at the time of my visit the cairn was obscured by recent forestry logging. The cairn was dug into in 1861 and two urns containing bones were found. All are now lost. Getting to the cairn is not easy. There is a track from the Lodge of Kilmichael Hotel, but I was turned back by machinery at Glenrickard farm. If you do negotiate this track, it ends at a rickety stile over a barbed wire fence. Fighting through the jungle of rhododendrons, bracken and briars brings you shortly to the ruined cottage. An alternative route is the 2½ mile (4km) long forestry road that runs between Cnoc na Dail car park on the Brodick-Lamlash road, and Gleann Dubh. About two thirds of the way along there is an unsignposted gate on the right (east). The wide forest track from here leads directly to the cottage.

Somewhere in the upper reaches of Glen Cloy is supposed to be a green mound known as Tornanshian. I think this may be the grouping of moss-covered boulders immediately adjacent to the footbridge over the Glencloy Water (NR994341) where the path from Auchrannie meets the forestry track from Cnoc na Dail at Gleann Dubh, but I cannot be sure. Earlier writers thought this was a fort or camp associated with Robert the Bruce's sojourn on Arran – Mackenzie MacBride, for example (*Arran of the Bens the Glens and the Brave*) says Bruce waded up and down the burn to disperse his scent when bloodhounds were hunting him, and other writers identify it with the 'stalward plas' in 'ane woody glen' where Bruce camped before taking Brodick Castle. Which he didn't take. All these Bruce associations are, I'm afraid, just fantasy. Tornanshian means 'the Mound of the Fairies', but I can find no associated folklore. Boyd Scott, writing in 1919, says that the fairies lived on 'the Fairies' Knowe near Elder Kerr's House'. This may be Tornanshian, or it may not be. South of the head of the glen is the peak known as Sithein (pronounced 'shee-an'), which translates as the Fairy Hill (NR999328).

CORRIEGILLS

The Isle of Arran Heritage book records the memories of nonagenarian William Hamilton, who lived his entire life at Dhunan in Corriegills (NS042350). He remembered two men who lived in the caves nearby. 'Andy' was a real recluse – men sailing past on the coal smacks used to call out and make remarks to him. The other cave-dweller was 'John Bell', reputedly a member of the Bell whisky family substantially reduced in the world. He scratched a living selling old baskets and posies of

East Mayish standing stone, above Brodick, looking north to Goatfell.

dyed white heather to the tourists. He also played the melodeon. Tilda, his wife, sold bootlaces. Mackenzie in *The Book of Arran 2* notes that fairies were often seen around Corriegills burn. Someone anonymised just as G-------- saw them dancing on a stone there. The top of a granite boulder on the site was flattened by the fairies dancing on it. Judging by what Mackenzie's source said – that only the bravest folk would go along the burn at night, for fear of baukans (bocans) – belief in the supernatural infestation of the area was genuine.

THE FAIRY GLEN AND LAG A' BHEITH

For walkers intent on getting to Lamlash an alternative to the unappealing main road is the path south from the centre of Brodick through the Fairy Glen. Facing the post office, take the curving road uphill to the left then turn right (south) to follow the signpost for 'Lamlash 3 miles'. After the static caravans you come to a crossroads of tracks. To see the impressive East Mayish standing stone★ (NS01813551) turn left for about 220yds (200m). The stone can just be seen from the curve in the track. This tall, narrow monolith is 10ft 10ins (3.3m) high. If you want access to the boggy field in which the stone stands, ask permission at East Mayish house. Back at the main track you continue climbing, reaching the eponymous trees of Lag a' Bheith, the Hollow of the Birches.

The book *Isle of Arran Heritage*, published by the Arran Heritage Community Group, has a piece of folklore related by Matt Smith (the interview was conducted by pupil Kim Robson). There was a prophecy that one night a certain man would meet Satan above the Cordon, at the south end of Lamlash. The man took with him a dog and a dagger as protection against supernatural evil. A bargain was struck – the man would perform a certain (unspecified) task and in return the Devil would tell him where in Lag a' Bheith a box of gold was buried. Another meeting was arranged, but the Infernal One insisted that this time the man had to leave his dog and dagger behind. The man duly turned up for the next rendezvous without the forbidden items. After the man completed the favour for the Devil, he was in return handed the directions for the gold. Satan then cackled and vanished, clearly believing the man's soul was his. But in the interim the wily man had secretly sought a protection spell from a wise woman, and he was safe. As pre-arranged he met the villagers in Lag a' Bheith, and they feverishly dug at the specified spot. A storm grew, but they ignored it. At the moment the chest was found, a great fiery rock burst out of the thunderhead and headed towards them. Everyone ran or buried their faces in the ground, trying to escape the Devil's vengeance for being cheated. When they eventually looked up the entire landscape had been changed beyond recognition. Thick clumps of birch were all around and they could not find the spot with the gold. This explains why Lag a' Bheith has such a great number of birch trees. The path now climbs the slope, the part between the birches and the road being known as the Fairy Glen (NS017342).

This name appears to have been bestowed by visitors in the first part of the twentieth century, and, as there is no other fairy folklore recorded in the area, may be related to the encounter with the group of little men on THE BRODICK TO LAMLASH ROAD (see the LAMLASH chapter, which also has details of the stone circle on the summit of the road). The path passes through a car park opposite the stone circle, then the Cnoc na Dail car park (which gives access to the forestry route to GLEN CLOY) and thereafter descends through woodland parallel to the road, ending at the first house in Lamlash.

2

THE STRING ROAD, GOATFELL AND THE NORTHERN MOUNTAINS

The String – so-called because from the sea it looks like a piece of string laid over the mountains – is the B880 road that crosses the high central part of the island, between Brodick and the West Coast. Buses run regularly along this route. This chapter covers first The String and then the mountains north of the road, including Goatfell.

THE STRING

Close to the first car park on The String is a badly-ruined cairn (NR98633605). The *Name Book* of 1864 states: 'Many cartloads of stones have been removed to build the parapets of the bridges on the Brodick-Shiskin road.' To the west of the 768ft (234m) summit on The String is Gleann an t-Suidhe, the Glen of the Seat, the eponymous 'Seat' being Suidhe Challum Chille, St Columba's Seat, where the great saint supposedly had a rest. This is one of the few placenames on the island associated with Columba; there is no evidence he was ever here. If there was ever a feature or monument on the site, it is long gone.

Domhnull (Donald) nam mogan from Tormore was returning from Brodick via Gleann-an t-suidhe when he met a spirit or creature called a bocan. Donald was told to return the following night but leave behind what he currently had on his person. He consulted a wise woman on the west coast. She told him to make the rendezvous but to retain the things had had been carrying – a sword, a Bible and a darning needle. On her advice he described a circle on the ground with the point of his sword, then stood in the middle with the holy book. The bocan was unhappy and accused Donald of having consulted the wise woman, to which Donald freely admitted. 'Well,' said the bocan, departing, 'had you done as I told you last night, you would never have seen your home again.' The story is told in *The Book of Arran 2*. For a variant on the same story of 'Donald and the Bocan', see MACHRIE MOOR.

A small serving of prehistoric monuments stand to the north of the road, close to Monyquil farm. Monyquil Chambered Cairn (NR94073526) is a damaged but substantial long cairn almost 100ft (30m) in length. You can just about make out the chamber. About 27yds (24m) north is a large 8ft (2.4m) high standing stone (NR94073529). A similarly sized stone lies flat 50ft (15m) to the west of the cairn (NR94043525). It may be a fallen menhir, or a capstone from the cairn. *The Book of Arran 1* reports on the 'Serpent Mound', a supposed ancient place of ritual near to the farm. An excavation in 1909 showed it was a natural esker (a mound of earth and stones left behind by a retreating glacier).

A curious red sandstone letterbox, decorated with carvings, stands at the junction of The String and the minor road from Machrie. The story, as related in *Isle of Arran*

Heritage, is that originally there was a white letterbox on the spot. The laird's daughter came riding by and the white stone gave the horse a fright, so the laird hired a stone-mason from Ayrshire to build the strikingly carved replacement. If you will pardon the contradiction, there is no obviously cryptic meaning to the symbols.

The remainder of The String is on low-level ground most easily accessed from the WEST COAST, and so is covered in that chapter.

GOATFELL

One of the popular routes up Goatfell passes through Glen Shant, with Glenshant Hill to the west (NR991395). Currie's *The Place-Names of Arran* gives the derivation as the Gaelic word *seunta,* meaning charmed, enchanted or sacred, and suggests there may have been a chapel or sanctuary here. James Robertson, in his *Tour through some of the Western Islands, etc.,* of Scotland in 1768 says, 'In Glenshant is a tomb or large chest near 12 feet long, and on its side is a man described in armour. This was lately discovered when digging peats. It has never yet been opened.' If either the tomb or chapel were ever here, they are present no longer.

Possibly the most unusual postbox in the country, on the String road.

THE ARRAN MURDER

On 4 August 1889 the body of Edwin Robert Rose was discovered on the east shoulder of Goatfell. The corpse had been hidden beside a boulder and screened off with an impromptu wall of rocks and stones built up with pieces of turf and heather. The head had been smashed in.

Rose had been missing since 16 July. A search party of upwards of 200 men had been scouring the hostile terrain for more than a week. William Roughead, whose works *Twelve Scots Trials* and *The Trial of John Watson Laurie (The Arran Murder)* form two of the key sources for the case, described the reasons for the difficulties facing the searchers:

> Upon the north and west Goatfell is bounded by a congregation of jagged mountain ridges and fantastic peaks, with deep shadowy glens and grim ravines, the bleak sides of which are furrowed by innumerable gullies and abrupt watercourses; a scene in its awful solitude and grandeur so wild, dreary, and desolate as hardly to be matched in Britain.

It was only the smell of decomposition that had ultimately led to the discovery of the body.

Rose had last been seen climbing the mountain in the company of a young man called Annandale. Subsequent police investigations established three salient facts: Annandale had skipped lodgings in both Arran and Bute without paying the rent; he had been seen with clothing, luggage and other items known to have belonged to Rose; and John Annandale was in fact John Watson Laurie, a pattern-maker at Springburn Works, Glasgow, who was clearly now on the run. A nationwide manhunt ensued, and press interest was intense. In a bizarre twist Laurie, possibly inspired by Jack the Ripper's taunting the police through the newspapers, wrote two letters to the press proclaiming his innocence. The first, posted to the *North British Daily Mail* on 10 August, and postmarked Liverpool, said:

> I rather smile when I read that my arrest is hourly expected. If things go as I have designed them I will soon have arrived at that country from whose bourne no traveller returns, and since there has been so much said about me, it is only right that the public should know what are the real circumstances... As regards Mr Rose, poor fellow, no one who knows me will believe for one moment that I had any complicity in his death... We went to the top of Goatfell, where I left him in the company of two men who came from Loch Ranza and were going to Brodick.

On 27 August another letter, this one postmarked Aberdeen, arrived at the *Glasgow Herald*, protesting about the 'many absurd and mad things' written about him and stating that, 'Although I am entirely guiltless of the crime I am so much wanted for, yet I can recognise that I am a ruined man in any case, so it is far from my intention to give myself up.'

On 5 September, after almost five weeks on the run, Laurie was arrested near Hamilton. The trial at Edinburgh caused a sensation, but the prosecution case for the actual murder was weak, with medical experts disagreeing over whether Rose's injuries were from a fall or an attack. There was no blood on Laurie's clothes when he was seen later that evening, and smashing someone's head in with a rock should have left extensive blood splatter. It was clear Laurie had robbed Rose, but had he murdered him? The jury found Laurie guilty by just one vote. The sentence was death by hanging, quickly commuted to life imprisonment, and Laurie spent the rest of his life behind bars, dying in Perth Prison in 1930. Edwin Rose was buried in the graveyard at SANNOX. The boulder marking his grave frequently bears various small memorials and tributes.

Many writers have re-examined the case and the general conclusion is that Rose died in an accidental fall – or possibly was pushed. There was certainly no close assault with a rock, no smashing open the face. Whether fall or push, Laurie did not go and get help, but robbed the body, hid it from view, and set off, rather dim-wittedly, in an attempt to enjoy his spoils. Laurie's conviction and sentence was therefore most likely a miscarriage of justice.

The most Fortean aspect of the whole case came during the cross-examination of the police witnesses. It turned out that, following the post-mortem, which was held in Corrie, the police constable, on the orders of his sergeant, removed Rose's boots, took them to the shore, and buried them below high-water mark. None of Rose's other clothing was taken; just his boots. The counsel for the defence wanted to know why this had happened, and pressed the subject hard, but both constable and sergeant refused to elucidate. The answer was obvious: the burial of the boots was an apotropaic act designed to prevent the dead man's spirit from 'walking'. There was, however, no way two West Highland Gaelic coppers were going to admit that in a court full of upper-class Lowland gentlemen.

MOUNTAIN ANGELS

Journalist Bill Burt interviewed two schoolboys who had finally turned up safe and sound after being lost for twenty hours on the Arran peaks. They both told him they had 'followed the lady down the mountain.' Their saviour had been a slim young woman in a white frock who had appeared out of the mist and silently guided them over difficult terrain into the arms of the search party. The rescuers of course saw no woman in white. Burt, an angel enthusiast, concluded this was a clear case of angelic intervention. See www.newfrontier.com/2/angel-story.htm for the story. The online report is undated, but is probably from the 1990s.

Goatfell in winter.

3

LAMLASH AND WHITING BAY

THE BRODICK TO LAMLASH ROAD

There is a curious stone circle★ on the east side of the summit of the road between Brodick and Lamlash (NS01873342). In winter it can be seen from the road. Take the minor path (not the track) from the edge of the front of the car park. After a couple of minutes the circle is visible on the left, across boggy heather, with an outlying standing stone in the foreground. On 28 September 1861, having dug five stone circles in a day on Machrie Moor the previous May, James Bryce excavated this circle, uncovering a very small central cist only 2ft 2ins (66cm) long and 10ins (27cm) deep, dug into the bedrock. The cist contained fragments of burnt bone, flints and black earth. The weather was not kind, as noted in his report in the *Proceedings of the Society of Antiquaries of Scotland*. 'Exposed in this elevated spot to the full fury of the south wind and force of the pelting rain, our men could hardly keep their footing, yet did they work away bravely till I had fully explored the rude cist.'

Horace Fairhurst, in *Exploring Arran's Past*, says there were originally seven stones, and indeed there are seven now. But thereby hangs a tale: *The Book of Arran 1* has a pre-First World War photograph of the circle in open moorland with brilliant views. The accompanying plan clearly shows four stones, and the positions of the missing three. The three large uprights and the big fallen boulder are the original stones; the three smaller stones have been added some time in the twentieth century, by person or persons unknown. The cist is no longer visible. This is probably the site inaccurately described by McArthur in *The Antiquities of Arran*: 'By the roadside between Brodick and Lamlash there stand three massive blocks of red sandstone, which are said to mark the spot where the lands of three of the old proprietors of Arran met.' It is also the spot in *The Isle of Arran Mystery* where Lady Penelope and Parker find the fabulous ruby (see the chapter on ARRAN AND POPULAR CULTURE).

A. Boyd Scott's *The East of Arran* (1919) tells of a farmer and his friend who were travelling in a cart past the circle: 'All went well till they were passing by the strange stones that lie to the right of the road, an eerie place, faith, to be at in the mirk, but it was still day-light...' The horse stopped stock-still, snorting and shaking with fear. After much urging it finally galloped past. The men looked back, and saw:

> A great company of little brown men on the road and hanging on to the tail-board of the cart, and, even as they looked, the wee folk loosed the tail-board and dang it down with a clatter on the ground. Then off they went with great glee, holding their little fat sides, like folk that have heard the greatest joke in the world.

Stone circle at the summit of the Brodick-Lamlash road, site of an alleged encounter with fairies.

The farmer and his friend stopped the cart, replaced the tailboard, and proceeded to Brodick. *The Book of Arran 2*, published five years earlier in 1914, says the incident took place within the previous fifty years, and there were three not two men in the cart, one of who had related the incident to MacKenzie, the *Book's* author. There were 'several' small figures, who were between 12-18ins (30-45cm) high.

The wide forestry road leading east from the circle and the car park takes you to several prehistoric sites in the forestry blanketing the Clauchland Hills. Go past the sign to 'burial cairn and standing stone'. After ten minutes a signposted path to the right leads to Dunan Mor Chambered Cairn (NS02803315), a vegetation covered mound with an unusual Y-shaped chamber which is virtually impossible to see clearly. A difficult, sort-of-waymarked sort-of-path leads steeply downhill into the gloom of the forest to reach Dunan Beg Chambered Cairn (NS02673300). The cairn is again invisible under vegetation but the tall standing stone★ next to it is impressive. McArthur in *The Antiquities of Arran* writes that the stones from this cairn were taken to build the schoolhouse in Lamlash. Descending further, and negotiating several walls and fences, brings you to another good standing stone 1.8m high, in a field north of North Blairmore (NS02923279), with views over Holy Island.

Returning uphill to the original forestry track, the route to the east continues through the plantation. To the north is the hill of Dun Dubh (NS039341), home to a fairy cave full of treasure. An old man called Fullarton often visited the little folk, taking a stocking to knit as he sat chatting with them. Despite the conviviality he always took the precaution of keeping a darning needle in the collar of his jacket or carrying a sprig of rowan. On one occasion he forgot his protection and the cave nearly closed before he could escape. The tale is in *The Book of Arran 2*. The track finishes at a knoll on top of which is the small Dun Fionn (Fingal's hillfort) (NS04643382).

The fortifications are hard to make out – and clearly far too small for a giant like Fingal – but the views over the water to the mainland are very fine. From here you can retrace your steps to the car park or head south to Clauchlands and Lamlash, or north to Brodick. Just below the downhill path to Brodick is an outcrop of pitchstone, a tough volcanic glasslike rock often used for prehistoric tools and weapons instead of flint. Flakes have often been discovered in cairns, and it was clearly a valuable trade item, as some has been found as far afield as Orkney and Ben Lawers in Perthshire.

In 1768 James Robertson wrote *Remarks made in a Tour through several of the Western Isles and West Coast of Scotland* (although it didn't come to light until the late nineteenth century). In it he describes the arrowheads made of pitchstone, and notes the people have:

> The absurd and superstitious notion that they are shot by infernal spirits, and will affirm that they are shot so fast in the shafts of their spades that it required much force to disengage them. They call this stone the Elf-shot stone, supposing that it is from the cows receiving a wound by this stone that they become elf shot.

In *Arran: An Island's Story* Allan Paterson Milne quotes Bess MacMillan, MBE: 'There are many springs or fairy wells in Arran and it was a very common practise for sick people to send for a can of water from some particular well which the fairies had blessed. The water restored them to health. There was one on the Lamlash Road to Brodick called Babs Well. I was born in Lamlash and was once sent as a little girl for a can of pure water for my sick grandmother.' Babs Well may be the same as Bauchop's Well, on the east side of the road at NS026323.

LAMLASH

The medieval chapel of Kilbride★ (NS03223227) is reached via the minor road that branches off east from the hill road at the north of Lamlash (look for signs to the golf course, but go straight ahead when the course is on the left). The first record of the church is from 1357, and it was abandoned in the eighteenth century. When the east coast's main graveyard on Holy Island closed in the 1790s a replacement was clearly needed. Local tradition says that a bright gleam was seen flickering in the trees above Lamlash; the light led to the abandoned chapel. So Kilbride became the principal graveyard of the area because of a divine signal rather than, say, because it was already a holy place and there was land available.

The current ruination and overgrowth is so extensive that it takes a time for this place to give up its secrets. A monogrammed stone dated 1618 is apparently built into the east gable but the ivy has covered it. The interior of the roofless chapel is divided into two rooms. That to the east has several large upright gravestones whose inscriptions have been so effaced that they look for all the world like a line of standing stones. The western compartment is entirely choked by impassable vegetation. The north door, normally kept closed, was opened at baptisms 'for the escape of the fiend.' Several medieval cruciform gravestones, and other carved stones, were described in the nineteenth century but have all long vanished. John McArthur in *The Antiquities of Arran* gives the tradition of one such lost stone, carved with a kilted figure armed with a sword: the two lairds on Arran, Walter Fion ('the fair-haired') and Duncan Tait, were sworn friends. A mischief-maker called McNish wagered he could make them enemies, and told each laird that his opposite number was plotting to murder him. When the two men met on the shore a little north of Lamlash they both drew swords and attacked. The two corpses were buried in the one grave.

There is a skull and crossbones on the south wall and several of the gravestones in the churchyard have Victorian ornamentation such as birds, anchors, swords and doves. The monument to Archibald Hamilton and his crew, drowned on 11 September 1711, reads: 'Ye passengers who e'er ye are/As ye pass on this way/Disturb ye not this small respect/That's paid to sailor's clay.' My visit to this otherwise quiet spot was soundtracked by the ceaseless cawing of the resident crow, which added somewhat to the atmosphere of the broken and leaning stones stained with bright orange lichen. One of the curiosities of the adjacent modern cemetery is that some of the graves now have solar-powered lights, so that on a summer's night it is filled with small glowing balls, eerily reminiscent of the 'death lights' folklore of previous eras.

Being (along with Kilmory) one of the two principal churches on the island in earlier times, the 'moral discipline' sessions of the kirk were held here, and along with the endless litany of people guilty of not attending church, or of fornication, or of both, there are records of more interest. All can be found in *The Book of Arran 2*. Robert Stewart was summoned for calling Mary Stewart a witch. He agreed he did use the term, upon good grounds, as 'she frequently used charms, for healing of diseases.' On 3 June 1705 Mary herself was hauled before the session and questioned about witchcraft. She agreed she used charms but there was no fault because the words she used were benevolent and Christian. To demonstrate this she repeated her cure for migraine 'and other distempers of the head':

> Christ will raise thy bones
> even as Mary raised her hands
> when she raised the wail of lamentation towards heaven
> as she gathered the body of the bound One.
> Peter will raise, Paul will raise,
> Michael will raise, John will raise,
> Molais and Moling will raise
> The bones of thy head up out of the flesh

Note that along with the conventional invocations (Jesus, Mary, the apostles) she also invoked the local saint, Molais (Molaise, see HOLY ISLAND) and another West Coast holy man, Moling (Molingus, see THE BAUL MULUY on HOLY ISLAND). The session, 'after holding furth to her that all charms proceeded from the Devil's invention, let the words be never so good, and that they were expressly forbidden in the word of God,' sentenced Mary to make public confession of her guilt at the next Sunday in front of the congregation.

On 28 June 1713 a goodwife named only as 'E.S.' from Blairmore told the session that when the women of the town were milking cows together, they talked about an apparition which had been seen recently by several people. According to E.S. 'Katrine K.' then said the apparition was 'the spirit of some person deceased who left some money hid, God send it my way to inform me where the gold is.' The next day Katrine verbally abused E.S., so the woman fired back that Katrine 'was a poor wretch who for the love of gear [money] prayed God to send the Divell in her way to inform her of money or a treasure.' Katrine admitted the original wish but said she spoke in jest. Nevertheless she was censured. Looking back through the records, it appears this was just one of a great many disputes about cows and grazing that had been ongoing within the womenfolk of the area, with incidents dating back at least a year earlier. This was the first time a ghost or anything supernatural had been mentioned, and probably served as just a good excuse for E.S. to attack Katrine.

James Robertson, on his tour of 1768, reported: 'lately were discovered by Mr Gershom Stewart, Minister in Kilbride, the Druids' instruments for sacrifice, such as brass wedges for cleaving their wood, an axe, and a brass flesh fork.' There is no other record of these items, whatever they may actually have been.

In 1896 a Viking burial was discovered at Millhill in the Margnaheglish area of Lamlash (NS03353189). Fragments of a sword and shield-boss were recovered. Haakon Shetelig, in his monumental work *Viking Antiquities in Great Britain and Ireland* (1954) writes that the artefacts were from no later than the middle of the eighth century, 'a surprisingly early date for a Viking burial in Scotland.' In *Exploring Arran's Past* (1982) Horace Fairhurst says he was told by the late John Sillars that a pile of about fifty skulls was found while digging the foundations of a 'back house' on the west side of the burn near the shore road just behind the Viking grave. The skulls were dumped in the bay. The story cannot now be verified. If the report was genuine, were these skulls the remains of a massacre? A displaced cemetery? Or a Celtic head cult?

The Book of Arran 2 retells a very old story told of the witch of Clauchlands. A ship said to be part of the Spanish Armada passed up the Firth of Clyde in full sail. The people had no cannon so they went in for alternative artillery, carrying the old woman to the shore in the hope that she could banjax the enemy ship. After watching the vessel for some time she said in Gaelic: 'There is on the top of the mast that which will suffice her.' What she had seen was the Devil in the shape of something like a large cat sitting on the masthead, and knew the ship was doomed.

On 25 April 1829, the brig *Caledonia* left Lamlash for Canada, carrying eighty-six islanders who had been forcibly cleared from North Sannox. A memorial of three huge stones stands on the green in front of Hamilton Terrace, in the centre of the village. On the other side of the road a small grassed-over mound contains a stone from the house of each person who went on the boat. Their minister preached his last sermon on Arran from the mound. A little further south on the seafront an unusual carved cross stands outside the current parish church★ (NS02563093). The weathered carving shows Christ emerging from a chalice as at a mass, with a kneeling devotee below. The reverse is a cross decorated with foliage. In an article in the *Proceedings of the Society of Antiquaries of Scotland* for 1908-09, J.A. Balfour says that the tenant of the farm on Holy Island removed the cross from his land sometime in the 1850s or 1860s, and buried it for purpose unknown in Kilbride graveyard (see above). It was found again in 1896, and at some point transferred to its present location. Bill McLaughlin, in *Molaise of Arran*, calls it St Brigid's Cross and states, with no obvious provenance, that it originally stood at Cnoc na Croise on the putative Pilgrim's Way, and marked the point where pilgrims from the west of the island saw Holy Island first time (see THE ROSS for more on the Pilgrim's Way). Below the cross is a hollowed-out stone, long believed to be a font, but probably just a mortar.

South of the church, and between it and the new high school at NS024308, a walled area of scruffy woodland is the site of the White House, once a grand mansion which was allowed to decay and was eventually demolished in the 1970s. All that remains

Right: Lamlash parish church – old cross with Christ emerging from a chalice, and mortar below.

Below: Lamlash – ruins of the outbuildings of the White House. Somewhere near here a ghostly horse and woman were encountered.

are the roofless ruins of the piggery, and some parts of the walls of the garden and stables. In the nineteenth century the foundations of a small castle were discovered in the grounds when a drain was being dug. This was probably the tower described in an account from 1543, said to defend the important harbour of Lamlash. The sea was certainly further inland than it is now, which would make this the right site. There is nothing to see of these foundations and they may have vanished completely. Maureen Smith, a founding member of the drama club and a Lamlash resident since 1974, told me a number of incidents relating to the White House and the neighbouring area. Just before the demolition took place the club were allowed to take anything from the house, for use as props. On the first floor all the rooms were unlocked except one. One of the group shouldered open the door – to reveal a room that was in immaculate condition, with not a speck of dust in it, despite having been empty for years. The opening of the room had been strongly objected to by another of the men in the group, who the moment it took place had dashed downstairs and out of the building. It transpired his mother had been a chambermaid at the house, and the room in question was known to be the haunt of the Grey Lady. Her apparition would be seen at the window, and objects would be found in a different place to where they were put.

In the mid-1970s Maureen lived in Park Terrace, behind the school and the area of the White House. Three workmen rented rooms from her for a while. One evening they wanted to go for a drink at the Auldersyde Hotel on the seafront. Two of them left together but the third was delayed by fifteen minutes, so he took the short cut through the White House woods. Just a few minutes later he returned, his face ashen, and went straight to bed, despite it being only early evening. The following day he told Maureen what he had experienced – first he heard a neighing sound, which gave him the creeps, as it didn't sound like a normal horse. Then in the distance he saw the form of a woman in a filmy, floaty grey dress. When she disappeared he took to his heels. He was not from the island and knew nothing about the Grey Lady or about the other spectre supposed to haunt the site, the headless horse.

Lamlash Community Hall was built in 1915 as a hospital for soldiers recuperating from wounds received in the trenches of the First World War. In 1959 it was gifted to the people of Lamlash, and served the usual community functions of dance hall,

Lamlash – former community centre, site of spooky happenings.

meeting room, cinema – and theatre. The drama club used it for more than three decades. Maureen Smith recalled an extensive series of strange incidents that had taken place at the hall over the years. All were concentrated in the backstage area, props cupboard and side door, on the west side of the hall (to the right when looking at the front of the building). On three successive nights Alan Little, the caretaker, locked the mortice lock and placed the two slip bolts on the side door – only to find the door open the following day. Several people, including Maureen's young son and a female member of the drama club, had an uncomfortable 'feeling' in the area, and tried to avoid going there. On one occasion, at Eastertime in the early 1980s, fifteen members of the club were having a meeting in the smaller room at about 7.30 or 8.00 p.m. when Maureen and one or two other people felt a cold draft – 'like a freezer door opening' – coming from the closed door of the creepy area, across the room, and past them. Shortly afterwards several people heard footsteps – as of a man with a slow, heavy gait – in the adjacent main hall. Immediate investigation showed there was no one there.

In 1986 or 1987 Maureen's son Jonathan was on an electrical apprenticeship and was working in the hall with his boss: when they stopped for lunch, they both heard footsteps in the main hall, which was empty. During a drama festival in perhaps 1999 the hall was full during a particular production, and Maureen, a friend who lived in Inverness, and that friend's then partner, David, were standing against the wall. David looked puzzled and said to Maureen, 'See that wee man standing against the back wall?' Neither Maureen nor her friend could see anything. David said the man 'was not from this time' and was dressed like a turn-of-the-century farm worker, with dark trousers and jacket and a shirt with no collar. To David he appeared absolutely real. Afterwards he went to the area of the hall – where other people had had bad feelings – and reported that he thought there was an old well or another underground water source there. The hall is situated behind the new school. It was scheduled for demolition in 2008 – perhaps this event will reveal more about the site.

In 2005 a prehistoric cemetery was discovered on a playing field that was due to be developed for the new Arran High School (NS023307), behind the White House site and next to the community hall. Four stone-lined cists were found, along with several inverted cremation urns containing burnt human bone. Other finds included pottery and a flint blade.

Maureen Smith also mentioned two other incidents in Lamlash. Her current home in Murray Crescent has a large garden which backs onto some trees. When her son Simon was about eight years old – this would be around 1982 – he was playing in the garden when he came rushing into the house, saying there was a man over by the trees looking at him. Maureen's first thought that it was a (possibly dodgy) visitor staying at the nearby caravan park, but it was off-season and the place was deserted. So she asked her son more about what the man looked like and what he did. Simon replied the man looked at him and then walked away, and described him as wearing 'a long brown thingy with a belt and a pointy hood'. 'Like a monk?' asked Maureen. 'What's a monk?' replied the boy. When it was explained to him he agreed that was what the man looked like. Before the incident Maureen had had a feeling she was being watched from the trees, but had not mentioned this to Simon. She had also heard stories about Altachorvie Hotel in Lamlash – where the father of a family staying there had died – where there were reports of objects having been moved around, and the sound of invisible children.

Driftwood goddess, next to Studio 4, Lamlash.

Metal heads, next to Studio 4, Lamlash.

In *The Antiquities of Arran* John McArthur describes how a small green tumulus was removed some years ago beside the Cordon, the southernmost part of Lamlash: 'It is said that an old sceptic to ghostly superstitions, in spite of warning and remonstrance, carried away the stones of the mound for the building of a house for himself and family; but though he toiled for days at the work, he could make no progress; some unseen agency continued to demolish the walls as they were being built, and he was forced to relinquish the impious undertaking.' The *Book of Arran 2* reports the case of a farmer, still alive in 1914, who remembered his father buying a calf which turned into a cow of such good quality that the factor bought it for himself. Early one morning, with all the neighbours watching the departure of the factor's cow, father and son set off to drive the animal to Lamlash. Before leaving they removed the apotropaic rowan knot that was always attached to her tail. Very soon the cow became sluggish, and then lay down and, irrespective of any prompting, would proceed no further. Two men came to help but could do nothing. Then the sister of one of them brought a vessel filled 'with a potent and disagreeable liquid termed in Gaelic 'Fual'' and poured it over the cow, which instantly stood up. The party went home, tied the rowan knot to the cow's tail, and next morning, unhindered by witchcraft or fairies, took her to Lamlash without difficulty. For a meeting with the Devil at the Cordon, see FAIRY GLEN in the BRODICK chapter.

WHITING BAY

In his 1919 book *The East of Arran* Boyd Scott related an experience told to him by Archie McMillan. Archie was driving home in his cart from the mill at Monamore in Lamlash to Whiting Bay. From the description he may have been using the old route over the hill rather than the current shore road, which was built in 1843. Archie had a presentiment something would happen. Earlier a bird had given an uncanny hoot. It was dusk, a liminal time. At an eerie spot where the road goes down the brae to the stone bridge over the Achancairn burn (possibly NS040278) the mare stopped dead and refused to move. The horse was quaking and in a cold sweat, and would not respond even when the whip was applied. On the bridge Archie saw a quiet blue flame like a corpse-light. A pale figure stood by the light, like a maiden, but 'of a deadly beauty'. Archie felt the cold fear up his backbone and his hair stand up. He cried, 'On I will go, I tell ye, though I drive horse and cart to the Bottomless Pit!' Out went the light, and the 'Fay maiden... melted away like a puff of mist over a dyke on the hill'. Archie charged safely across the bridge and heard a splash in the burn far down below, 'like the sound of a great monster slipping back again into the water.'

In *Arran: Behind the Scenes* Gillean Bussell gives a slightly different version, although the essential details remain the same. Here, though, the man was returning from a night's drinking, the bridge was called Bocan Bridge (a bocan being a spirit) and as the horse and rider eventually rode over it the monster was heard to shriek as it fell into the water below. Bussell also suggests the tale was created to warn off excisemen.

Scott has another tale of the supernatural from this area. A young girl, walking in the high fields above Whiting Bay in summer, plucked a posy of heather, harebells and clovers. As she sniffed it the waters of the Firth of Clyde became transformed into a land of beauty and flowers and distant bells. The girl was about to run to this magical land when she was stopped by a misshapen old woman who snatched away the posy. The vision vanished and so did the witch. The disappointed girl found the posy on the ground, entire except for the magic clovers which give sight of the Otherwordly paradise, known variously as Innis Eabhra, Tir-na-Og or Hy Braisil. For more on Innis Eabhra, see CORRIECRAVIE.

For Kingscross Point★, pass the church at the north end of Whiting Bay and follow the road, then the track, past all the houses of Sandbrae. Ignore any signs to Kingscross, as this takes you to the hamlet of that name, not the Point. From the final turning circle walk along the edge of the beach until you come to a signpost that says 'Kingscross Point 1 mile'. Follow this through woodland and over a couple of stiles. From here the possible paths multiply and, just when you need them, the signs disappear. As a general rule, always go right, which will keep you parallel to the shore until you eventually reach Kingscross Point. An alternative and shorter route comes from the road-end via the Kingscross side road.

The Point (NS056283) is home to a triple monument★. Firstly the path runs right through a boat-shaped hollow which is indeed a Viking boat burial. A woman was laid under an upside-down boat and the whole edifice set on fire. Finds included iron rivets and nails from the boat, some melted pieces of bronze and a few fragments of a whalebone plaque. The boat-grave may have been placed over an older cairn. Next comes a small dun, possibly Iron Age, with a substantial rubble-filled outer circular wall some 20yds (18m) across and 4yds (3.5m) thick. Hearths, charcoal and burnt bone were found during an excavation in 1909. Then comes what looks like a standing

Kingscross Point – the controversial standing stone with its cairn, and the dun in the background.

stone set in a modern four-sided cairn. The stone's age is uncertain. The *Name Book*
of 1864 suggests the stone stood alone at 6-7ft (1.8-2.1m) high but the RCAHMS
record won't commit itself: 'It is possibly a Bronze Age standing stone to which a later
tradition is attached, but in its present state this is conjectural.' This 'later tradition' is
the sticking point, as it refers to the belief that the stone was erected to mark the spot
where Robert the Bruce embarked for the mainland (hence 'Kingscross'). The story
is told in Barbour's medieval metrical epic *The Bruce*, although the exact place is not
given.

It was 1307 and Bruce was starting to make his comeback from defeat and exile to
victory and the crown, but the odds were against him. Bruce had sent a messenger
to Carrick on the mainland with the instruction that if it was safe to return he was
to light a beacon on Turnberry. The country was occupied by the enemy so the messenger did not light the fire. Someone, however, did set something burning, probably
farmers getting rid of pease straw, and seeing the supposed signal Bruce decided to
set off. While his men were preparing the boats Bruce met a woman on the shore. It
was in her dwelling at Whiting Bay that he had spent the previous night (and which
was yet another proposed location for the encounter with the persistent arachnid).
The woman prophesised to him:

> Within short time ye shall be king,
> And have the land at your liking,
> And overcome your foemen all

Bruce thanked her, but was not quite convinced, supposedly saying:

> Indeed it is wonderful, perfay,
> How any man through stars may
> Know the things that are to come,
> Determinedly, all or some

As we know, everyone in the Middle Ages spoke in verse. Bruce went on:

> But me think it were a great mastery
> For any astrologer to say
> This shall fall here and on this day.

In other words, he didn't quite believe her. She, however, was so convinced of the
truth of her prophecy that she sent two of her sons to fight for Bruce: 300 men then
rowed across to the beacon, where they met the messenger, who was full of fear as the
fire was not his, and the country was hostile. Despite misgivings they went on, and
after seven years' fighting Bruce regained the throne of Scotland. Note that Barbour
was not an eye-witness to the events and some of *The Bruce* is romantic recreation (or
propaganda, if you will).

All of this means that the standing stone may be a Bronze Age monolith to which
the tradition of the Bruce has become attached, and the cairn has been built up by
sympathisers, sentimentalists and tourists. Or, the stone was indeed put up in post-
medieval times to commemorate the event. McArthur, in *The Antiquities of Arran*, also
says: 'in a neighbouring field, there is an unhewn block of sandstone, believed to be

the sole relic of the rude cot in which the King resided, on the eve of his departure from the Island.' This stone cannot now be identified.

The Bute Rock in Whiting Bay was named after a sailor who came ashore and was caught thieving: 'there was a little pinnacle of rock on the brae-face behind, to the back of the old post office; the irate Arranites hanged him there and put his name on the rock – the 'Buteman's Rock'.' The source is an undated article called 'Old Arran – Forgotten Tales', written by Malcolm Sillars for the *Ardrossan & Saltcoats Herald*. The copy is in the Arran Heritage Museum.

The *Book of Arran 2* has its usual crop of local folklore. In the 1860s the blacksmith prescribed the eòlas-cronach for a horse that would not eat. The eòlas (spell) was obtained from a wise woman near Whiting Bay, and contained water, salt and a large needle, although it may also have had other things. The cure was placed in a wooden ladle and sprinkled on the animal's shoulders, ribs and hips. Then a part of the hair from each sprinkled area was burned with a lighted candle. The candle was passed under and over the beast three times starting near the shoulders and ending at the hips. A person stood on each side, and the candle was handed from one to the other, completing the circle. The horse duly improved. The witness who related the episode was a boy at the time. One of MacKenzie's respondents (MacKenzie being the main author of *The Book of Arran 2*) said that as a child he was taken on a visit to his father's relatives, who lived south of Whiting Bay. Getting into the gig to go home, the old grandmother brought out a farl of oatcake and broke it over him as he lay sleeping in his mother's arms. This was an apotropaic ritual designed to protect the child from the fairies.

According to Boyd Scott (*The East of Arran*), fairies lived on the knoll where the Smiddy Road meets the high road at Whiting Bay. This may be the area now show on the map as 'Fairy Glen'.

Glenashdale at the south end of Whiting Bay has a splendid 1½ mile (2.5km) circular walk, starting along the south side of the burn up to the waterfalls*, and back via an Iron Age hillfort. The signpost is on the south side of the bridge at the southern extremity of Whiting Bay. After a few hundred metres a path to the left (south) is marked to the Giants' Graves Chambered Cairns* (NS04292467 and NS04302463). Note that the climb up involves a long set of steep steps. Other than the name there is no folklore associated with the sites, which are damaged but evocative 'horned gallery graves', the 'horns' being the arc of the façade that faced onto the semi-circular forecourt and framed the entrance to the inner chamber. They are the largest Neolithic tombs on Arran. Excavation of the greater, northern cairn in 1902 by Thomas Bryce uncovered pottery fragments, three flint knives, four leaf-shaped flint arrowheads and a large amount of burnt human bone. The entire floor was covered in black earth containing pieces of charcoal. The second cairn is about 60ft (18m) south of, and at right angles to, the northern cairn. The Hunterian Museum, Glasgow, holds six stone axes whose provenance is given as 'the Giants' Graves chambered cairn,' with no other details.

Another chambered cairn, Torr Loisgte, hides in the woods at NS04042477, below the summit of Torran Loisgte. It's not easy to reach as there is no direct path. Go into the trees behind the Giants' Graves and find a narrow track. After about 10yds (9m) turn right at a T-junction, then after 20yds (18m) turn right again, at another T-junction. Follow the track for a few hundred metres until you come to small hillock. Go round this to the left and continue in a north-westerly direction for another few hundred metres. This last section is the worst, and you may have to divert into the trees to avoid the bog, but the mound is visible as a target in the distance. Note that extensive forest logging operations in the area in early 2008 may have changed some of these directions.

The cairn was not discovered until the mid-1970s, and is in a reasonable state, largely due to its elevation and its obscure location deep in the forest. At least one smaller cist is built into the rear of the monument.

To the south is the tree-swamped hill of Cnoc na Comhairle, the hill of counsel (NS036240). John McArthur (*The Antiquities of Arran*), calling it Knocklecarleu, Consultation Hill, says this was in tradition where chiefs from various tribes met when threatened by invasion fleets.

About 50yds (45m) past the junction with the route to the Giants' Graves the Glenashdale path passes, on the left, the site of a tiny medieval chapel (NS041252), now a barely-noticeable mound with a few unidentifiable stones just poking through the rank grass. Silver coins were found in one of the graves in the nineteenth century. The falls were once known as the Falls of Kiscadale ('coffin dale'), 'Kiscadale' probably being derived from the graveyard of this largely undocumented chapel. The path now proceeds upwards, the edges of the Forestry Commission fir plantation being fringed with ancient deciduous trees whose fantastically-shaped trunks and branches are completely coated in vivid green moss, giving the walk a sense of enchantment. The best view of the falls themselves is from the projecting wooden platform on the north, from where you can clearly see the double cataract, and the cavity behind the lower falls which, theoretically, allows you to pass behind them, although if you descend into the pathless almost-vertical chasm to do so, on your own head be it. The falls are best viewed after heavy rain.

A further 200yds (180m) on, on the northern side of the falls, the path brings you to a signposted Iron Age hillfort, with the walls on two sides still partially intact and a spectacular drop preventing attack from the south. Follow the path away from the river and hopefully, amid the confusing pseudo-paths, you will encounter an obvious forestry track. Turn right. If after 300yds (275m) you cross a ford you're on the right route. Continue out of the forest and into Whiting Bay.

Standing stone near North Blairmore, with Holy Island in the background.

4

HOLY ISLAND

Holy Island or Hōly Islċ is one of Arran's most enchanting and intriguing places, with St Molaise's early Christian hermitage and medieval pilgrimage site, striking modern rock paintings, caves, wildlife (or at least, feral-life) and, like everywhere on Arran, good walking and scenery. The ferry service is via a small boat from Lamlash, run by Tom Sheldon (telephone 01770 600998 or mobile 07860 235086). If you are planning on exploring the island take an early ferry, as there is a great deal to see.

The island has gone through a welter of names. The earliest recorded name may be Inis Shroin, 'the island of the water spirit'. The Vikings called it Melasey. In 1263 it provided shelter to the galleys of King Haakon of Norway prior to, and after, the Battle of Largs, which saw the start of the decline of Norse power in the area. In 1549 Dean Munro called it Yle of Molass, after St Molaise (of whom much more to come). In Gaelic it was known as Eilean Molaise, Molaise being pronounced MO-LASH-EH. This became corrupted into, variously, Elmolaise, Lemolash, Lamalasche or Lamblash Island. Pont's map of the late sixteenth century shows 'Lamlach or Holy Yle'. Eventually the reworked Gaelic word migrated across to the mainland to become in 1830 Lamlash village, and the island's name became codified as the Holy Isle or Holy Island. The latter is that used by the Ordnance Survey.

THE LANDING AREA/THE CENTRE FOR WORLD PEACE AND HEALTH

The first thing that strikes you when you arrive at the landing point is the arc of colourful prayer flags and eight stupas★ (Buddhist structures used as a focus for pilgrimage and prayer, and found at holy sites). In 1992 the island was purchased by the Buddhist community of Samye Ling in Dumfriesshire, following a remarkable pair of parallel dreams – Lama Yeshe Rinpoche 'saw' the island when practicing dream yoga in the early 1980s, and in a dream in 1990 Mrs Kay Morris, co-owner of the island and a devout Catholic, was instructed by the Blessed Virgin Mary to pass Holy Island to the Lama, so that it could be used to promote peace and inter-faith dialogue. The Buddhist community has engaged in a vigorous ecological initiative, including the management of the wildlife (both indigenous and introduced) and an extensive native tree-planting programme. Some parts of the island are part of a nature reserve and are off-limits to visitors. Note that dogs should not be brought onto the island.

You will usually be met by a member of the community, who will explain what you can see and do, and answer questions on the activities at the island's Centre for World Peace and Health. For more on the Buddhist community, I recommend Kristine Janson's booklet *Holy Island*, usually available on the ferry and at the Information Centre.

Right: The Centre for World Peace and Health.

Below: Soay sheep with Buddhist stupas and prayer flags.

All the background information on the centre and the Buddhist rock paintings comes from this very informative publication.

The centre is essentially a place for retreats and residential courses, and is not open to visitors. Overnight accommodation is available for guests. In 1993 a cutting from the famous Fortingall Yew, from Glen Lyon, Perthshire (at 3,000 to 5,000 years old, the oldest living thing in Europe), was planted behind the centre. Other cuttings of this special tree were distributed by the Conservation Foundation to selected special places, such as Glastonbury Abbey. Next to the centre is the community's Mandala Garden*, a delightful open mini-labyrinth filled with small figures of fairies and gnomes and decorated with Buddhist figures and messages. Close to the garden are the tea room and information centre, located in a restored boat shed. This is the only place for refreshments and toilets on the island. In the area here you may well meet the Eriskay ponies, Soay sheep and Saanen goats, all of which live free and undisturbed, with no fear of humans. Please do not feed the animals.

The centre and the ancillary areas are built on a site with a venerable, if confused, history. The *Book of Arran 1* records the tradition of a monastery founded here by Reginald, Lord of the Isles, in the early thirteenth century. Other than brief notes in *The Book of Clanranald* (a manuscript compiled during the seventeenth and eighteenth centuries by the MacVurich family, the hereditary bards and seanachies of the Lords of the Isles and then the chiefs of Clanranald) and Munro's 1549 *A Description of the Western Isles of Scotland Called Hybrides* – which mentions 'ane monastry of friars which is decayit' – there is no other documentary record of the institution, and it may well never had existed as a monastery proper. In 1908 excavation revealed the foundations of a circular tower, which was probably the remains of a small defensive structure built by Somerled, first Lord of the Isles, in the twelfth century, and mentioned in a maritime defence account of 1543. A small fragment of the tower wall stood until 1879.

Built into the cliff above the farmhouse are the almost-vanished remains of what may have been a chapel, the tentative identification based solely on a note in Robertson's *Tour* of 1768: 'the remains of an old chapel, built after the Gothic taste'. More certain than any of these is the existence of a former graveyard, probably where the garden is now. Fairhurst, in *Exploring Arran's Past*, suggests that the proximity of Molaise's Cave may have led through association to the establishment of a cemetery, and then a chapel for pilgrims and mourners. In the same way that St Columba's reputation helped Iona become the 'holy island' destination for dead Kings, so too did the lingering sanctity of the hermit Molaise establish this site as the main cemetery for the people of Arran. Another factor in the choice of the island as a burial spot may have been the belief that spirits cannot cross water and would therefore not return to disturb the living. And, of course, there were no wolves on the small island to disinter the bodies. McArthur, in *The Antiquities of Arran*, states that the graveyard was in continuous use until about 1793, when a boat carrying a funeral party from Lamlash overturned and several people were drowned. The tombstones were removed in 1835 and onions and carrots planted on the site. Traces of the graves could still be seen in 1908, but there is nothing visible now.

The old farmhouse – now renovated as the centre – was in use until 1938.

Everyone knew about the miniature people who were said to appear in the kitchen of the farmhouse on Holy Island. One day, the small ferry brought to Holy Isle a lady and her granddaughter. She talked of these 'wee folk' and had seen them. The

Above and below: The centre's garden, with fairy locator.

lady had been born and brought up in the farmhouse and was returning to see the place of her birth.'

This story was told to Linda Taylor by her grandfather Bobby Taylor in 1991, and recorded in the Arran Heritage Community Group's book *Isle of Arran Heritage*. Bobby had been the ferryman who brought the old woman back to her former home. Hamish Haswell-Smith, in *The Scottish Islands*, records another tradition associated with the house. The farmer's wife bore him fifteen daughters. Angered at not getting a son, he murdered her and buried her body under the stone-flagged kitchen floor. This tale may well be entirely apocryphal.

On 27 November 1890 the *Ardrossan & Saltcoats Herald* published 'A Legend of the Holy Isle', written by someone known only as 'A.B.C.' It told the tale of a sea captain who lived on Holy Island with his wife and son. The boy's mother died and when the captain had acquired enough wealth, he married again. Returning from a lengthy voyage, he discovered his new wife had been starving the boy and hoarding the money. When the lad was of the right age he went off to sea, but not before the captain took him for a father-and-son chat on the beach. The old captain said at that moment he was carrying most of the gold he owned, but he did not want the boy's stepmother to get hold of it. So together they buried the gold on a hill. If the boy returned first he knew where to find money. If the father returned first he would add to the secret pile. But that year, both the father and son were killed on separate voyages. The mother died knowing nothing of the gold. And it is still there. Sadly, the article does not explain (a) if all the parties died, how the event was communicated to posterity, and (b) where the gold was actually buried.

The earth mysteries magazine *Northern Earth* (online at www.northernearth.co.uk) reported a curious incident from 1972. Pete Hannah and his wife were relaxing in the sun somewhere near the farmhouse when they heard a sudden loud buzzing, like a swarm of angry bees, which seemed to be coming from the very ground beneath their feet. The noise was sufficiently alarming for the couple to run away in fear, although no bees or any other insects could be seen. Years later, reflecting on this experience, Pete felt that perhaps having just spent a couple of hours sitting quietly in the sun in a beautiful location, their 'stilled' state of mind might have amplified their perception of the noise, and that as they became more afraid the buzzing (and therefore the perceived threat) seemed to get louder. 'Nature panic' has been reported by mountaineers, walkers, anglers and others who spend time outdoors in lonely places. In its literal sense, the term 'panic' comes from the Greek word *panikos*, which itself derives from the nature god Pan, and describes the fear and alarm that can sometimes be felt in natural places, even though there is no obvious cause. In such cases, people were said to have met Pan (even if they didn't actually see him in person).

A circular walk proceeds along the shore to the southern tip of the island, returning over the 314m (1,030ft) summit of Mullach Mòr ('big summit'), an exhilarating trek on a good day. Those less energetically inclined can proceed along the easy shore path as far as St Molaise's Cave or the lighthouse, and return the same way.

Approximately 300yds (275m) south of the centre, hidden at the foot of a low cliff, is the tiny Smuggler's Cave (NS05303031). With luck and a good torch you may be able to see sixteen small carved Greek crosses on the north wall. Before St Molaise's Cave you pass a sign to the Nyanang Belly Cave. This is a reference to the belly-shaped cave in Nyanang, Phelgyeling, Tibet where the important Buddhist figure Milarepa once sat in retreat.

St Molaise's Cave entrance, and the Norse runes on the walls.

St Molaise's Cave: two of the many carved crosses.

ST MOLAISE'S CAVE★★, HOLY WELL★ AND TABLE★

¾mile (1,200m) walk south of the centre along the raised beach brings you to this signposted rock shelter (NS05862972), the hermitage and pilgrimage site from which Holy Island receives its name.

Essentially the cave is a waterworn rock overhang in a sandstone cliff, facing east across the bay. At first glance it appears unprepossessing, but if you spend some time there its secrets gradually reveal themselves – especially if you visit later in the day, when the afternoon sun helps bring out the carvings. I have been greatly aided in identifying the carvings by the descriptions and diagrams in Ian Fisher's masterly *Early Medieval Sculpture in the West Highlands and Islands*.

Looking at the cave from the front, there is a rough set of steps on the right. Further to the right, on the cliff-face above the slope, is a Latin cross (a cross with a long lower shaft), with three triangular terminals, a D-shaped top terminal and a central ring. Left of this, on the sloping roof above the foot of the steps, are two simple crosses, followed by a larger sunken Latin cross with a smaller cross cut into the shaft. Moving further left there are numerous other small crosses. Then, at the north end of the cave, are three larger sunken crosses, amidst many smaller crosses both carved and scratched. Below this trio of prominent crosses, on different rock surfaces, are several sets of Norse runes. The pages of *The Proceedings of the Society of Antiquaries of Scotland* in the nineteenth century were filled with divergent translations of these, accompanied by the sound of distinguished scholars politely blowing raspberries at their learned but, in their minds, absolutely mistaken, colleagues. The readings given here are taken from Fisher, who himself is quoting from a standard work by M.F. Barnes and R.I. Page. The highest, and most obvious inscription, just below the central of the three sunken crosses, reads 'Vigleikr the marshal carved', this possibly being a chap called Vigleikr Prestsson, who was one of the leaders of Haakon's expedition of 1263.

Scattered above the runes are approximately fifteen simple crosses which appear to have been carved at the same time, possibly demonstrating that the Vikings came as pilgrims too. The other runes are on a rock level below this one. Moving from left to right they read: the personal names 'Ólafr' (Olaf) and Jóan (John); a single character, possibly the letter 'm'; the personal name 'Ámundr'; 'Onundr carved runes'; two sets, one above the other, the upper being undecipherable and/or damaged, and the lower reading 'Nikolas from Haen carved'; and finally, the personal name 'Sveinn' (Sven).

Just south of the cave and next to the path is the saint's holy well★, a pure spring currently thoughtfully provided with a ladle should you wish to drink. James Robertson in 1768 called it 'St Maolisa's Well, with a bathing pond, which the natives used to drink and to bath in for all lingering ailments.' McArthur in *The Antiquities of Arran* notes that this was a popular healing well: the water supposedly having miraculous properties, but no tales of healing have come down to us. McArthur also mentions that the saint's bath 'is within the tidemark of the shore below', although this has yet to be identified, and also that 'the cliff next to the hermitage is renowned for its carbuncle, but the gem is invisible if you approach it.' Modern additions to the scene include a small 'nature' shrine at the spring, and several columns of pebbles on the beach, similar to those found at DRUMADOON.

The most obvious feature, however, is St Molaise's Table★, a large, 7ft (2.1m) high block of sandstone with a leveled top, a few metres north of the well (NS05862970).

St Molaise's Well, with drinking ladle and offerings.

St Molaise's Table; one of the seats is visible on the right.

Four seats have been cut at the corners, and artificial steps and handgrips are evident. Cut into an angled rockface on the north-east corner is a small but deeply-cut cross with a ring on its top arm. No date can be assigned to it. Other than some kind of association with St Molaise's Cave and Well, it is not clear what the 'Table' has actually been used for, although folklore guesswork can be surmised from its alternative names – the Judgement Stone (with a possible association of sanctuary), the Pulpit Rock and the Saint's Chair. Boyd Scott, in *The East of Arran*, has a suggestion: 'possibly in savage times… the stone was the scene of justice among the Stone Age people, and barbarous executions, it may even be of human sacrifice.' Hmmm.

Beside the Table is a small block with a shallow basin. *The Book of Arran 1* thought it was probably a font, used for holy water. The RCAHMS 'Canmore' website sees this as just a natural depression caused by sea action, which 'is unconvincing as an antiquity'. And the Revd Kennedy Cameron, in *The Church in Arran*, with absolutely no evidence, considered it as a repository for possibly the most intriguing of all the lost items from Arran's magical past – the Baul.

THE BAUL MULUY HEALING STONE

I had like to have forgot a valuable Curiosity in this Isle, which they call 'Baul Muluy,' i.e. Molingus his Stone Globe: this Saint was Chaplain to Mack-Donald of the Isles; his Name is celebrated here on the account of this Globe, so much esteem'd by the Inhabitants. This Stone for its intrinsick value has been carefully transmitted to Posterity for several Ages. It is a green Stone much like a Globe in Figure, about the bigness of a Goose-Egg. The Vertue of it is to remove Stitches from the sides of sick Persons, by laying it close to the Place affected; and if the Patient does not out-live the Distemper, they say the Stone removes out of the Bed of its own accord, and è contra. The Natives use this Stone for swearing decisive Oaths upon it. They ascribe another extraordinary Vertue to it, and 'tis this: The credulous Vulgar firmly believe that if this Stone is east among the Front of an Enemy, they will all run away; and that as often as the Enemy rallies, if this Stone is east among them, they still lose Courage, and retire. They say that Mack-Donald of the Isles carried this Stone about him, and that Victory was always on his side when he threw it among the Enemy. The Custody of this Globe is the peculiar Privilege of a little Family called Clan-Chattons, alias MackIntosh; they were antient Followers of Mack-Donald of the Isles. This Stone is now in the Custody of Margaret Miller, alias Mack-Intosh: she lives in Baellmianich, and preserves the Globe with abundance of care; it is wrapped up in fair Linen Cloth, and about that there is a piece of Woollen Cloth, and she keeps it still look'd up in her Chest, when it is not given out to exert its qualities.

The writer is Martin Martin, author of *A Description of the Western Islands of Scotland circa 1695*. This detailed description gives us a green globular stone which was a guarantor of oaths and proficient in healing and battle magic, and which in the late seventeenth century was closely guarded by hereditary custodians. *The Book of Arran 1* expands this with a legend still current on Arran in the early 1900s. When St Molaise visited the sick he put the stone on the floor as he entered the sickroom. Its action it indicated the outcome: if it stayed stationary the sick person would recover; if it rolled out of the door, their death was certain.

What became of this remarkable object? In his *Tour* of 1768 James Robertson says, 'there is still to be seen here a Byrral, which the priests consulted always in the man-ner the Jewish high priest did his Urim. It is taken to be an oriental pebble.' (The Urim and Thummim were two objects used for divination and worn on the breast-plate of the Jewish high priest; their exact nature is unknown.) Is the Byrral the same as the Baul? The similarity of the name, the magical use described and its description as a 'pebble' suggest it is so. McArthur, writing in 1861, and referencing *The New Statistical Account* of 1845, says it had still been in use for man and beast 'by the present generation' until it was lost 'by a gentleman to whom it was entrusted, who partook too much of the skepticism of the present age to appreciate its value.' This all suggests the Baul was lost in the 1820s or 1830s.

In contrast, Mackenzie MacBride, in *Arran of the Bens the Glens and the Brave* (1911), noted that the Baul was still preserved in the safe-keeping of the Crawford family. The *Book of Arran 1* begged to differ, noting that Mr Robert Crawford did indeed have a healing stone which had been in his family for more than 200 years, but that it was not the Baul. The Baul is described as a green stone about the size of a goose egg. The Crawford stone, in contrast, was rock crystal, and smaller. One side was flat and oval, the dimensions being described as 48mm by 35mm (almost 2ins by nearly 1½ins), while the other egg-shaped, the extreme thickness 10mm (less than 0.4ins). The stone was broken slightly at one end, having accidentally fallen into a fire. There was no information about the last time the stone had been used, but traditionally, 'as soon as he [the healer] crossed the threshold of the house wherein the act of healing had been done, the first living thing that came in the line of his path died,' so it was customary to arrange for a sacrificial animal to be provided. On one occasion this was not done and the healer came across a man and four horses in Glen Scorradale, and they all dropped dead at once. For further detail on this death-dealing episode – which however does not mention the healing stone – see THE ROSS. *The Book of Arran* notes that the size, shape and nature of the material of the Crawford healing stone suggests it may have once formed part of a reliquary, 'and the virtue ascribed to it may, in the first instance, have been due to its association with the relics of some saint.'

On the face of it, the Crawford stone cannot be the Baul Muluy. But there is a final mention, in a typescript preserved in the archives of the Arran Heritage Museum, 'Postman's Journey', written in 1937 by Donald Stewart of Corriecravie. Stewart says the Baul was kept by Robert Crawford in Glen Scorrodale for many years. When Mr Crawford died in 1915 Stewart suggested to the heir – a nephew – that it should be given to the Arran Society of Glasgow, so it could be placed in a museum. The man concerned thought it was too valuable an heirloom to part with, 'so it is now somewhere in the neighbourhood of Liverpool.' Possibly the Crawford stone had simply been confused with the Baul. But whatever the identification, it is clear that Arran had one, or perhaps two, remarkable healing stones, now sadly lost.

ST MOLAISE AND ST MOLIOS

Who was St Molaise, and why is he little known outside Arran? Molaise was a Dark Ages holy man, although his biography has become clouded and partly mythologised – not to mention conflated with another saint of a similar name but of an entirely different millennium. For much of what follows in clarifying Molaise's story, I am indebted to Colum Kenny's *Molaise: Abbot of Leighlin and Hermit of Holy Island,* and Bill McLaughlin's *Molaise of Arran.*

Molaise was born in Ireland sometime between AD566 and AD573. Like many saints of the period, he was of royal blood. His mother, Gemma (aka Mathgemm), was daughter of Aedan, King of Dal Riata, the Irish kingdom established on the West Coast of Scotland. Aedan received his kingship in AD574 from the (equally royal) St Columba, the first time a Christian power-broker had been explicitly involved in choosing a monarch. Molaise's father was Cairell (aka Cairil or Cuinid), King of the Dal Fiatach and of Ulster and Man.

As was *de rigeur* for Dark Ages saints, Molaise's birth and childhood were garlanded with miracles. The newborn infant made the sign of the cross and the previously barren midwife became fertile; a blind man named Senachus had his sight restored after bathing his face in the child's baptismal water; Molaise's nurse, bitten on the hand by a deadly snake, was miraculously cured by the child.

His early years were spent in Dal Riata. At the age of possibly fourteen he was sent to be educated in Ireland by the holy and respected Fintan Munnu, a former pupil of St Columba. While there the miracles continued – water required for milling was found where there was none, and twice Molaise's prayers assisted travellers who had been attacked by pirates. In one case the criminals fell to squabbling over the spoils and killed each other, and in the second the pirates 'retreated as though they were being attacked, abandoned their boat and fled like madmen to their ships.' The quote is from the 'Salamanca Manuscript', a medieval hagiographical work on Molaise, much quoted in McLaughlin.

When he came of age, Molaise was offered the kingship of the Dal Fiatach and of Ulster and Man, but he refused, and instead set out on a Christian mission, first choosing to live on what would, as a result of his residence, become known as Eilean Molaise, the Isle of Molaise. He lived in this cave for around ten to twelve years sometime between AD 590 and AD 604. Arran may seem an odd choice, but actually it made perfect sense – it was a well-known stop on the sea-highway connecting Ireland and the coast and islands of the west of Scotland, and, as even holy men need back-up, Arran was conveniently under the protection of Molaise's militarily powerful grandfather Aedan, King of Dal Riata.

After his time as a hermit, Molaise visited the relics of the saints in Rome, was ordained as a priest and then as a bishop, and became abbot of Leithglinn in Leinster. The Salamanca Manuscript has more to say on the miracles from this period of his life. He restored a beheaded man to life (which puts him a notch above Columba, whose own resurrection of a corpse took place on a whole body). When negotiating over the land for the monastery at Leighlin, the owner's contemptuous offer was as much as could be covered by the abbot's cloak. The cloak went on the ground and miraculously grew to cover the exact acreage for a full set of monastic lands. And, as an insight into the saint's steely fundamentalist prejudices, when his sister, a nun, became pregnant by a monk, he cursed her to a death at childbirth; afterwards he refused to have her interred in consecrated ground and the body was laid in a bog. The young monk concerned undertook a massive recitation of the psalms and eventually saw his former lover in a vision, saying that as a result of his devotions she was almost saved. When Molaise finally saw angels rising from the grave he relented and had his sister reburied in the churchyard. He died in AD 639.

Unfortunately for us, there are no records of Molaise's activities on Arran. All that we have is the clear evidence that in the medieval period his cave became a place of pilgrimage. Robert McLellan, in *The Isle of Arran*, suggests that Molaise's lasting reputation may either be due to the location of the cave – on a bay often busy with ships, some of them carrying important and influential people – or, more likely, because, in the ecclesiastical disputes of the day, he championed Roman Church practices over Celtic ones. Eventually the Roman church totally eclipsed its Celtic counterpart, and, based on the principle that history is written by the winners, Molaise's reputation may have been boosted at the expense of earlier Celtic saints, who were deliberately neglected. Clearly he must have had some impact on the local population, but we are left to guess what that was – or to rely on traditions that are almost 1,000 years later than the saint himself.

Our saint's original Irish name was Laisren. As was common at the time, this was shortened and the prefix 'mo' added, this being an honorific term of endearment and respect, meaning 'my dear'. So Laisren became Molas, meaning 'my dear Las'. When naming the island after the saint, 'the Island of Molas' became not Eilean Molas (which is grammatically incorrect in Gaelic) but Eilean Molaise (pronounced mo-lash-eh). At this point we enter the murky waters of saint-name confusion, a subterranean world which has ensnared many a distinguished writer trying to make sense of the variation of written and spoken names. Martin Martin, as described above in the section on the Baul Muluy, writes in 1695 about St Molingus, 'Chaplain to Mack-Donald of the Isles'. The legend of the stone's healing properties clearly identifies its owner as St Molaise. Clearly a Dark Ages saint could not have ministered to the medieval Lords of the Isles. McArthur, however, writing in 1861 says Muluy/Molingus was Molocus, a favourite saint, whose Baculum More (big staff) was carried before the bishops of

Argyll. An early eighteenth-century healing charm that came to the attention of the kirk session at Kilbride includes the lines:

Molais and Moling will raise
The bones of thy head up out of the flesh

Clearly here Molaise and Moling (Molingus) are regarded as two different people (the full charm is given in the LAMLASH chapter). It is therefore possible that Molingus has no connection with Molaise other than a vaguely similar name. Or they could be the same person, with tradition confusing dates and conflating names. Or Molingus could be St Molios.

Thomas Pennant, in his *Tour* of 1772, goes into great detail on St Molios, who he regards as the same as Molaise, but whom some later writers, including Balfour in *The Book of Arran* and McLaughlin (*Molaise of Arran*), are convinced is a completely different man, who operated several hundred years later (probably in the thirteenth century) and in a different area (the west of Arran, not Holy Island). Molios is derived from Maol-Iosa, 'the tonsured one for Jesus'. It may be a generic name that could be applied to any monk, and has been attached to the medieval effigy of an ecclesiastic in SHISKINE.

Pennant also adds the detail that St Columba visited his pupil Molios on Arran (there is no evidence the two ever met; the tradition may have been invented to explain the two place names named after Columba on Arran, or the tradition actually created the place names). Pennant's style was to write down verbatim what he was told by the people he met; he had no way of checking possibly spurious local tradition against historical reality. Unfortunately, Pennant's work then came to be used uncritically by later writers. McArthur, for example, in his influential but not entirely reliable *Antiquities of Arran*, takes Pennant at face value. Headrick compounds the tale with more flights of fantasy and his own prejudices (at the time Headrick was writing, Protestant authors took every opportunity to attack the supposed corruption of the early Church): 'the traditions in Arran state that Molios, disgusted with the [sexual] irregularities of his master [St Columba]… took up his residence in a cave in the island of Lamlash… it appears that, after he had made many converts in Arran, he removed to the district of Shisken, where he died at the advanced age of 120 years.'

For years, writers have, following Pennant, confused saints Molaise and Molios, because on the page they are similar, and there are sufficient other variations (Molos, Molash, Maolisa, Maeljos, Melios) scattered across various works to justify the conflation. But we are definitely dealing with two separate individuals. Molaise was a reasonably well-documented Dark Ages saint who lived on Holy Island in the last decade of the sixth century, while Molios, although not mentioned in any surviving documents, was most likely active around about the thirteenth century and was based in Shiskine. (Probably.)

As for Molingus, he was either Molios… or Molaise… or, more probably, someone different altogether.

THE SOUTH OF THE ISLAND

About 130yds (120m) south of the Table, and east of the path, is another sandstone block with three hard-to-find weathered crosses. The largest is 6ins (16cm) high.

Above: Rock painting of Green Tara.

Right: Rock painting of Marpa the Translator.

Left: Rock painting of the first Karmapa Dusum Khyenpa, with shrine.

Below: The Buddhist mantra OM MANI PEME HUNG painted on a rock by the shore.

From hereon you see a number of rock paintings★★ of figures from Tibetan Buddhism. With their bright colours and striking expressions they are an amazing sight in the heather and boulders of the sombre Scottish landscape. All were carved by a Tibetan monk living in Samye Ling. Most are accompanied by prayer flags and shrines of stones, shells, glass and other small items, and sometimes with more elaborate temporary structures. In the order you encounter them, from north to south, they are:

White Tara, then Green Tara – two aspects of the same female deity. White Tara is associated with long life, Green Tara with the overcoming of fear and obstacles. Both are dedicated to protecting beings from suffering.

Marpa, the Translator (1012-1097) – the first Tibetan patriarch of the Kagyu Lineage: the oral transmission of teachings from teacher to disciple, from the Buddha to the present. His forbidding expression reflects his tendency to give his students virtually impossible tasks.

Gampopa (1079-1153) – student of Milarepa (see below). He founded the first monastery in the Kagyu Lineage. Bright red clothes and headwear.

On a boulder west of the path, a series of coloured Tibetan characters forming the phrase OM MANI PEME HUNG, the most widely used of all Buddhist mantras. The literal translation is something like, 'the one who holds the jewel and the lotus,' a combination of compassion and wisdom.

Buddha Shakyamuni (560-480BC) – Siddhartha Gautama, the man who became the Buddha. Hair of blue, face and body of gold.

Dusum Khyenpa, the first Karmapa (1110-1193) – golden halo, red clothes, black and orange hat. Gampopa's most gifted student. He predicted his future incarnations, all of whom would be known by the title 'Karmapa'. The Karmapa is the head of the Karma Kagyu Lineage. Before each Karmapa dies, he leaves the details of where, when and to whom he will be born in his next life, so the lineage can recognise him. Miraculous signs accompany the birth. The current Karmapa is the seventeenth in his line.

Milarepa (AD1052-1135) – a student of Marpa. He achieved enlightenment after meditating for years in remote caves in the mountains. White clothes with a red sash.

The 'cave' marked on the OS map at NS061290 is actually two adjacent caves set back from the path in a natural basin enclosed by a dry-stone wall. The first cave is a rock shelter with a curious triangular entrance, but the second is a vulva-shaped cleft just one person wide, echoing with dripping water, going into the rock for maybe 20m. Bring a torch. And no hint of claustrophobia.

At the southern end of the path is the automatic lighthouse and associated buildings, the latter now the Inner Light Retreat, home to women on a traditional Buddhist three-year and three-month long retreat. Naturally, it is off-limits. The letters of OM MANI PEME HUNG are painted on the stones of the wall-dyke. The path now passes the private track to another building up the slope – the entrance marked by a smaller rock painting – and continues to a junction. Going right takes you to the east coast and the second lighthouse, close to Dorothy's Well (NS068292). The origin of the name is unknown. From here you have to retrace your steps as there is no path through the nature reserve. Turning left at the junction takes you up to the summit of Mullach Mòr. The trig point on top is often festooned with prayer flags. The path runs north over the wild terrain of Mullach Beag and eventually steeply down to the centre and the jetty.

5

THE ROSS ROAD

This chapter follows the narrow, high level minor road from Lamlash to Sliddery. The short southern low-level part of the Ross, from the main road at SLIDDERY/ BENNECARRIGAN to Glenree Mill, is covered in the chapter on the south coast. Note that other than the occasional post bus there is no public transport along this route, and that it can be a challenging drive in winter.

The damaged, but worth visiting, chambered cairn known as Meallach's Grave★ (NS017288) is on a pleasant circular walk from the Forestry Commission car park at Dyemill, near the start of the Ross. Note that, as of January 2008, all the serried ranks of forestry conifers around the cairn have been felled, to be eventually replaced by new plantings of Scots pines and broadleaved trees. The open, exposed hillside now presents a different prospect, and an entirely different walking and navigating experience.

From the car park ignore the main forest track and turn right at the sign marked 'Lagaville Walks – Figure of Eight 1 or 2 Miles Long Circular Trails', shortly after the path splits, with each route following one side of the burn. You can take either, but where they connect again at a wooden bridge further upstream, make sure you turn west (white arrow). Ignore the signpost to Urie Loch. Continue up the slope until you reach a small sign announcing the site of Lagaville, a settlement voluntarily deserted in the nineteenth century, when its residents moved to the bright lights of Lamlash. Very little is left, and the ruins are difficult to make out. A pond, dug in the 1990s, lies opposite. After a few more minutes there is a signpost to Meallach's Grave to the right. Up until recently the cairn lay in a clearing surrounded by forestry, but now it is obvious on the open ridge above you.

The three-compartment chamber is open and the pair of portal stones are gen-uinely impressive – one being almost 8ft (2.4m) high. The curving frontal façade can be made out. Monamor, as the site was then called, was excavated in the early twentieth century by Thomas Bryce, who found very little. In 1961 (now known as the Monamore chambered tomb), it was excavated again by Euan MacKie, whose investigations of the forecourt produced twenty-four areas of charcoal, 128 pieces of pitchstone and several pieces of Neolithic pottery. Dating analysis showed that the cairn was constructed around 3900BC and was in use for about 1,200 years until it was finally blocked up around 2700BC.

As far as I can tell the site was renamed 'Meallach's Grave' as a result of a competi-tion run in the local school, although I have not been able to determine why this name was chosen. There is no entry for an individual called 'Meallach' in any of the standard works on Celtic and Gaelic sources. As an adjective it means 'beguiling' or 'bewitching', but the context is wrong. I am tempted to think it is a version of either Meargach or Miach, both characters from Irish myth. The former, Meargach of the Green Spears, was killed by Oscar, Fingal's grandson; Oscar himself is said to be buried

The portal stones and
chamber of Meallach's
Grave chambered cairn.

at SLIDDERY, so there is an Arran connection. Miach was killed out of jealousy by
his father, Dian Cécht, the god of medicine; 365 herbs grew on his grave – so the
'grave' element may be the key here.

Return either the way you came or alternatively via the main, if rather boring,
forestry road. If you take this road south-west (to the right), or directly from the car
park, it allows you to visit AUCHELEFFAN STONE CIRCLE and CARN BAN
CHAMBERED CAIRN (see KILMORY). A mountain bike is the best transport, as
it's a long walk.

The Ross climbs through Monamore Glen to the car park at the summit. John
McArthur (*The Antiquities of Arran*) says that a huge cairn of stones somewhere near
here marked the coffin resting place for funeral parties taking bodies to the highly
revered burial site at SHISKINE. There is no trace of the cairn now. In January 2008 a
single, solitary tree here, in the middle of nowhere, was still decorated with Christmas
tinsel and decorations.

The south-eastern part of the Ross, descending to Sliddery Water, is Glen
Scorradale. Glenscorrodale farm, the childhood home of the former Scottish first
minister, Jack McConnell, is now a Buddhist retreat for men (the female retreat is
on HOLY ISLAND). Ronald Currie's *The Place-Names of Arran* gives the prosaic
etymology for Scorradale as Norse, *Skar*, a deep gully, but *The Book of Arran 2* tells us
it is from Scorri, the resident giant. He habitually annoyed the women who trekked
through the glen to sell their butter and eggs at Lamlash. Eventually the harassment
got too much and two bands of men stationed themselves at either side of the pass
where the ridge was steepest. When the giant appeared one group shouted 'Scorri,
Scorri' and taunted him with cowardice. Enraged, he ran up the hillside. Then the
other lot started jeering, Scorri turned around and chased them up the other side.
When he arrived at the top he was so out of breath the humans easily overcame him.

Bill McLaughlin in *Molaise of Arran* suggests that there may have been a medieval pilgrims' way to the north of the Ross, starting in Shiskine, passing west through Clauchen Glen, and thence visiting Cnoc a' Chapuill (Hill of the Chapel, NR969300), Cnoc na Croise, (Hill of the Cross, NR973314) and the adjacent Lag na Croise (Hollow of the Cross), before descending down the Benlister Glen to Lamlash. Although the names are suggestive, and McLaughlin mentions a folk memory of some sort of pilgrimage route, there is no strong evidence for the way, so for the moment the suggestion is unproven.

It is a commonplace of stories involving magical actions that, for one benevolent act to succeed, a sacrifice must be made to keep the universe in balance. When it came to healing on Arran, the sacrificial victim was the first living thing on which the eye of the curer fell. *The Book of Arran 2* tells of Seana bhean Thorralin, the old woman of Torrylin. She had effected a magical cure in Lamlash and was on her way home. When she reached Corriehiam (NR955265), now a ruin by the side of the road, west of the abandoned farmstead of Gargadale, she met a relative, William McKinnon, ploughing with his son and four horses. She knew what would happen but could do nothing to avoid it. All six fell dead. The plough was not touched and was left in the unfinished furrow. It is said that about 1884 the irons of a wooden plough were found on the spot where tradition said it happened. William lived about the early eighteenth century. For a variant on the story, in which the cure was effected through the use of the rock-crystal healing stone in possession of the Crawford family, see THE BAUL MULUY HEALING STONE on HOLY ISLAND.

The *Book of Arran 2* also mentions that a man was travelling by cart on the Ross Road when his horse froze and would go no further. Its ears stood up, and it was snorting and sweating with fear. A small cloud or mist arose and grew larger until it reached a great size and took on the form of a wraith. We are not told what transpired, only that the man 'had met this thing more than once'. The ghost was one of several Fingalian heroes who had died in a battle nearby; recent agricultural work had disturbed their rest, causing their spirits to walk. It is possible these supposed graves are among the large number of prehistoric monuments that dot the boggy upland area north of Glenree Farm, some of which were only recorded in the 1990s or even later. Glenree means 'the King's glen' and is supposedly named so after Oscar, Fingal's grandson (for more on Oscar and his 'grave', see SLIDDERY). The nature of the terrain and the sheer quantity of stones means that the exact location of all the sites is confusing, and you may find some remain elusive (especially when the bracken is growing), whereas others you will stumble across accidentally. The best starting point is the path that runs north from the farm road towards Clauchan Glen and Pien. For the first mile (1km), the Allt Burican burn is to the east of the path; once a ford has been crossed, the path runs between the Allt Burican to the west and the Allt Cul Corriehiam to the east.

The most obvious feature is a prominent standing stone at NR94592679, approximately mile (1km) north of the ford, and just to the east of the path. This faintly cupmarked stone is almost 5ft (1.45m) high, and acts as a useful marker. Just to the north at NR94592715 there is a small stone 2.5ft (0.8m) high. If you look across to the west, another similar stone can be seen on the skyline 635yds (580m) away at NR94592678, and there are two more, further east, in the next valley along. These diminutive stones are almost certainly boundary markers. In summer you'd be hard-pressed to find any of them.

About 100yds (95m) up the slope to the north-east is a small 'four-poster' stone circle (NR94672685). Look around and you'll find two more circles. West of both the path and the Allt Burican (NR94142685) is the very damaged façade of a Clyde-type cairn. Considerably to the north-east of the marker stone, on the boggy land towards the Allt Cul Corriehiam and Cnoc an t-Seabhaig, are two small possible standing stones (NR95092737 and NR95122728), although the former at least is probably a glacial erratic. In the immediate area are several hut circles. East of the road, just below the summit of Torr Beag, are three pairs of large stones. It is not obvious what they are, but they could be a monument with ritual sexual significance, as one stone of each pair is tabular, and the other pointed. (For more on prehistoric male-female sexual symbolism in stone circles, see MACHRIE MOOR). The stones are on the 220m contour at NR95772518, NR95652524 and NR95682530.

Some folklore motifs are, with slight variations, repeated right across Scotland, and the following, related in *The Book of Arran 2*, is a good example. A farmer was riding home one night from Lamlash to Clachaig along the Ross. As he passed through a dark lonely hollow something jumped onto the horse's back behind him, and just as quickly leapt to the ground. The horse bolted, but this made no difference to the entity, which repeated the action several times. At last the farmer seized it and bound it with a leather belt. At home he found it was a monster, one of a group 'which were a source of terror to the neighbourhood.' He tied it to a forked post which supported the rafters of the loft, but soon the creature's mother turned up, intoning threateningly:

Wet and cold my beard,
Put my darling outside,
Or the highest stone in thy house
Will soon be the lowest

The farmer wisely released the sprog and heard the maternal scolding: 'I hope you have not revealed to them the virtue of egg-water or the root of the nettle.' Ronald Black's 2005 commentary on John Gregerson Campbell's folklore classic *The Gaelic Otherworld* says that water in which an egg had been boiled was regarded as a love charm – throwing it over the object of desire bound them to you. Black gives an example from Mull, where if an unprepossessing girl had acquired a handsome swain, the expression was 'she has put the egg water upon him'. What is meant by 'the virtue of the root of the nettle,' however, eludes me. For another example of magical egg water see BENNAN, where the entity involved is named as a brownie, although elsewhere in Scotland the mischievous creature is identified as one of the tribe of hairy anthropoids called urisks. Boyd Scott, writing a few years later in *The East of Arran*, says the 'Thing', as he terms it, was human-shaped, but cold, slimy and hirsute, with webs between its fingers, and hair like an otter's on the back of them. When Ma Urisk turned up, her rhyme went:

My beard is cold and wet,
Give me back my pet,
Give me back my bairn,
Or I'll turn thy house into a cairn!

When the farmer released the brat he heard a cry like a mare makes upon her foal, and then the sound of padding away.

6

THE SOUTH COAST

LARGYBEG

> We are told that the upturned bones lay for many months scattered around, and that over them the ghosts of the desecrated dead wandered by night amid fitful gleams of lurid light! (John McArthur, *The Antiquities of Arran*)

McArthur was referring to 'a large number of stone coffins' destroyed by ploughing in a field near Largybeg, although from other of his descriptions he may have been confusing the site with Largymore and the GIANTS' GRAVES to the north.

The two standing stones at Largybeg★ (NS05372332) are worth a visit if only for the spectacular setting overlooking the sea, with a view south-west to Dippin Head and north to Holy Island. The deeply pitted stones are just over 3ft (1m) and 4ft (1.3m) high, and stand prominently on a small headland, usually shared by some curious cows. Just what this site actually is, nobody seems to be sure. Is it the remains of a burial cairn? An actual setting of standing stones? Horace Fairhurst in *Exploring Arran's Past* even expresses his doubts that the place is prehistoric at all. And there is no explanation, either folkloric or historical, for the traditional name – the 'Sailor's Grave' or 'Sailors' Graves'. Fans of alignments may note that the two stones seem to be on a line between Holy Island and Ailsa Craig. On the edge of the cliff, 50yds (45m) to the west at NS05332330, is a small cairn.

To get to the site, take the route marked 'footpath' just to the south of the houses at Ford (do not walk through the houses themselves) then turn right at the track and descend to the stile on the left. It's about 500yds (450m). Note there is no parking at the start of the walk, which is on a dangerous bend. From the site there is a signpost for an alternative footpath, north along the shore to Largymore, although this is challengingly muddy.

DIPPIN HEAD

McArthur in *The Antiquities of Arran* tells us that a tunnel supposedly leads underwater from near Dippin Lodge (NS04962233) to Ayrshire. A piper and his dog went in but never returned. The entrance may possibly be the sea-worn cave on the shore. *The Book of Arran 2* expands the story. The piper was called Currie; he could be heard far underground playing 'Currie will not return; the calves will be cows before Currie returns'. Can you really derive that degree of information from a bagpipe skirl? Currie

A pair of standing stones at Largybeg, with Holy Island in the background.

was never seen again, but the dog emerged – without any hair – not in Ayrshire but in Cantyre in modern Kintyre, that is, on the part of the Scottish mainland opposite the west – not the east – coast of Arran. That's some tunnel. The 'Piper in the Tunnel' motif is almost universally distributed around Scotland, and the 'hairless dog returning from underground peril' theme is also widespread; for an example, see KING'S CAVE.

KILDONAN

This attractive village is reached by a steeply-descending minor road which loops along the shore before rejoining the main road up an equally-sharp slope. The name derives from St Donan or Donnán, for whom there is moderately reliable documentary evidence that he was martyred in AD617 on the island of Eigg. There is no evidence for his presence on Arran. Local tradition, however, has Donan buried beside the mill wheel on Kildonan Farm (NS035212). J.A. Balfour in *The Book of Arran 1* describes seeing the foundations of a chapel on the roadway and lawn leading to the farmhouse. In about 1907 four long cist graves were found 12yds (11m) to the east of the chapel site, but were built over. A little to the south was a spot called 'The Priest's Grave', but nothing was visible. It is possible that the chapel may have been dedicated to Donan, and this, combined with the presumed early Christian graves, may have given rise to the tradition that the saint was buried here.

The ruin of the square tower of Kildonan Castle★ is an obvious landmark on the eastern end of the village. It is in a private garden and has been declared unstable and is therefore too dangerous to enter, but an excellent close view can be obtained from the adjacent track, where there is also an interpretation panel. Its history is murky, having had a number of owners, but it may not have been fully rebuilt after being burnt by the Earl of Sussex in around 1558. Along with BRODICK CASTLE and KINGSCROSS at Whiting Bay, it is one of the suggested locations from which Robert the Bruce watched for the Turnberry beacon in 1307. Purely on the grounds of line of sight, I consider KINGSCROSS has the edge.

The castle's last recorded use was as a cobbler's shop. The book *Isle of Arran Heritage* by the Arran Heritage Community Group says there is a legend the third step had treasure buried beneath it. A short circular route connects the castle, the beach, and the small standing stone at NS03372086, by the small car parking space between the castle and the hotel. This stone is a curiosity. The RCAHMS 'Canmore' website notes an 1864 report in which the site is described as being a raised mound, with a second smaller stone, and the comment, 'giving the appearance of the remains of a stone circle'. The *Book of Arran 2* also says 'remains of a circle'. There is nothing on the present site to support this, and the second stone is unknown.

The Kildonan Hotel has a real surprise – an arthouse version of a stone circle★★. Nine varied concrete structures are arranged around an octagonal tiled patio inset with geometrical designs, one of which gives the illusion of a shadow. Eight of the pieces are finished in pink and grey, but one is a very 2001-like black rectangular monolith. Six of the 'stones' are punctured with circular, triangular or wave-like holes, while one looks like a kind of magnet and another is leaf-shaped. Close by are a large ship's anchor and propellor.

Arthouse stone circle, Kildonan Hotel.

PLADDA

Nobody has lived on this low-lying island since the lighthouse became automatic. The former lighthouse mechanism and light is kept at the ARRAN HERITAGE MUSEUM. Pladda (NS0219) was once home to a medieval chapel dedicated to the fourth century St Blaise, martyred by the Roman emperor Diocletian using an iron comb. In legend, the giant Scorri (see THE ROSS) dug out a shovelful of rock from the moors and threw it into the sea, thus simultaneously creating Pladda and Loch Garbad (NS019240). Pladda is where, in *The Isle of Arran Mystery*, the assassin Hawkins finds the clue hidden in a seal's skull (see the chapter on ARRAN AND POPULAR CULTURE).

AILSA CRAIG

This great rock can be clearly seen jutting out of the Firth from anywhere on the south coast of Arran and also from the Ardrossan-Brodick ferry. It is often called Paddy's Milestone, although another name recorded is Creag Ealasaid (Elizabeth's Rock). Ailsa Craig may be derived from the Gaelic Aillse Creag, meaning fairy rock. It is the second largest breeding area in the world for gannets.

Considering its remoteness and inhospitable topography, the island has a number of interesting residues of human occupation. Up above the lighthouse is the ruin of an old castle tower (NX023995). There is no reliable history for it, but the three stars of the Hamilton coat of arms on a stone suggests it was built by or for the Hamiltons for some purpose. The monks of Crossraguel Abbey may have used the site as a retreat, or as a place of penance. The *Ardrossan & Saltcoats Herald* for 30 May 1884 reported that excavations for the gasworks for the lighthouse had uncovered two ancient graves, about 3ft (1m) from the surface, covered with stone slabs. A portion of a leg bone was found, but the other bones were much decayed. The slabs were 250ft (76m) from the tower, which was supposed to be the site of the monks' chapel. The report went on: 'to this sanctuary popular legend likewise has attached a graveyard, where is concealed a fabulous amount of golden treasure.' Whether the graves were shipwrecked sea men or monks, 'is and probably will for ever remain, a mystery, together with the hidden treasures of popular imagination.'

Hamish Haswell-Smith, in his fine book *The Scottish Islands,* gives a concise recent history of the rock, as well as noting its features of interest. In the nineteenth and twentieth centuries a small population of quarrymen and their families lived on the island, which was noted for producing curling stones. The workers brought in rabbits to supplement their diet. Brown rats arrived in 1889 when ships were ferrying materials and supplies to the newly built lighthouse. The quarrymen later claimed that the rats and rabbits were interbreeding, presumably creating rabb-rats. The rats made serious inroads into the resident bird population and were only finally exterminated in 1991.

The rock has several caves, including one on the south-west coast described as a 'mini Fingal's cave', and others called Macanall's Cave, Swine Holes, Swine Cave and Dalton's Cave. There are also two disused foghorns, an old anchor in the beach, a rusted narrow-gauge railway, a forge, and quarried waste granite pieces, 'from which the spheroidal curling stones have been cut leaving fascinating shapes like miniature Henry Moore sculptures'. Ailsa Craig can be visited on occasional boat trips from Girvan, Ayrshire.

AUCHENHEW

Back on Arran, a footpath from the car park where the road from Kildonan rejoins the main road leads north to Eas Mòr waterfall★: a magnificent sight. *The New Statistical Account* says that this cascade 'occasionally presents a phenomenon of singular and beautiful appearance – an iris, perfectly circular in form.' Louis Stott in *The Waterfalls of Scotland* supports this, writing that in certain weather conditions, a brilliant rainbow hangs over the falls, acting as a landmark for sailors, although I haven't seen it myself. To the east of the falls is Columbkille, one of the three placenames on Arran referencing St Columba, who was also known as Columcille. I can find no tradition regarding the name.

Ronald Currie's *The Place-Names of Arran* mentions Torr an Fhiannaidh, the hill of the giant or Fingalian, further inland in the area of the hills Cnoc na Garbad (NS025237) and Cnoc na Feidh (NS014252), but I cannot find it on the Ordnance Survey map.

LEVENCORROCH

East of Levencorroch farm is a small thin standing stone 2ft 8ins (81cm) high. *The Book of Arran 2* describes a second, broken stone, and the possibility that this was a stone circle. *The Name Book* of 1864, quoted on 'Canmore', notes that Mr W. Shaw of East Bennan claimed the walls of a chapel stood during his grandfather's time at the roadside near the junction to East Bennan. It was called 'Caibeal Mhuineal' and had still been used as a burial ground within living memory. *Caibeal* is chapel, *Mhuineal* might mean neck. Nothing remains now. The site is given as NS00002137.

BENNAN

Best approached along the beach east from Torrylin or west from Kildonan, the Falls of Struey★ and the Monster or Black Cave★★ (NR993203) together make a terrific destination for an easy but energetic walk below the heights of Bennan Head. The waterfall cascades over 50yds (45m) of cliffs down to the shore. Immediately to the east is the sea-worn cave, the largest on Arran, a single space 80ft (24m) high, 40ft (12m) wide and 100ft (30m) deep. This is one of the few caves in Arran where you do not need a torch, as the mouth is huge and the space is well lit. There is also a sizeable opening at the rear which leads to a natural chimney, although this is something of a dead end unless you are a gecko.

Prehistoric arrow-heads and flint flakes, mingled with whelk and limpet shells, were found here in the nineteenth century. Writing in 1861, McArthur (*The Antiquities of Arran*) says the cave was used for church services until recently. This must have been very uncomfortable, as the floor slopes steeply and is strewn with boulders, and the vast mouth of the cave is open to the elements, including the spray from the sea. Gillean Bussell (*Arran: Behind the Scenes*) claims that travelling people lived in the cave below the high-water line where rents were not required to be paid. Note that it is easy to be cut off by the tide here. At high tide you will not be able to pass the headland of the cave and will either have to retrace your steps back the way you came or attempt the near-vertical thorn-clad slope above.

The Black or Monster
Cave, looking south
to Ailsa Craig.

Just west of the cave mouth are two small ceramic heads★★ cemented to a rockface. They can be easily spotted from the large upstanding rock with a small 'hat' on the top, to the north-west. I have no idea why they are there or who constructed them.

The alternative name for the Black Cave is the Monster Cave. The tale is given in Francis Thompson's *The Supernatural Highlands*, where the report is dated to 1895. The 'monster' was a Gruagach, a kind of female brownie who looked after the cattle and was rewarded with libations of fresh milk poured onto a hollowed stone. This golden-haired Gruagach herded the cattle in the township of Bennan and did her job so well that 'no spring loss, no death loss, no mishap of disease ever befell them, and they throve, fattened and multiplied'. She would wait on a hillock for the cattle and controlled the herd with only a pliable reed, with which she switched at those who annoyed her. She was also known to swear mightily. Off duty, she liked to sit in the sun and sing. The report gives her two homes, Uamh na Gruagaich, the Gruagach's Cave, and Uamh na Beiste, the Monster Cave. I am unable to tell if they are the same or different locations.

The Book of Arran 2 carries another tale which is so similar in some respects to the first that it may be a variant – or perhaps it is a different story altogether, with both having only the location in common. A long time ago a Mèileachan arrived at Bennan. This was a creature neither man nor beast, also known as a Bleater. Mackenzie says it was the young of the Glaistig, who was 'a thin grey woman dressed in green, a mortal endowed with the fairy nature, who is attached to a house.' The creature associated himself with three of the largest farmers at Bennan, and went out with the cattle every day. His head and body were always covered, and only his legs were visible.

Two views of the pair of ceramic heads near the Black Cave.

Each morning he was out early, shouting, 'The cattle of Cook, the cattle of Mackinnon, the cattle of Big Ferguson of Bennan – turn them out.' One cold winter day one of the women found him shivering and moaning with cold. She put her own plaid over his shoulders. As is traditional in brownie stories, the gift compelled him to leave. Crying out, 'Ill is the turn thou hast done me, and heavy is the burden thou has lain on me,' he left weeping bitterly, and was never seen again.

Yet another tale was associated with a family on an unnamed farm in the south of the island. *The Book of Arran 2* tells how the brownie had lived at the farm for a long time, working with the cattle and sleeping in a cow-stall in the byre. He was never seen to eat, but each night the goodwife would throw a handful of meal in the pit hanger above the damped-down fire, and it would be found licked clean in the morning. Then the son of the house married. One cold day his young wife, taking pity on the creature, threw an old coat over him. Immediately he burst into tears and was compelled to leave. The old wife of the house said, 'I care not whatever if he does not tell two things – what virtue is in the root of the burr, and what substance in the sweat of an egg.' This is the same strange phrase used in an encounter with a supernatural being on THE ROSS, where water in which an egg had been boiled was regarded as a love charm, although 'the virtue in the root of the burr' remains unexplained.

The Book of Arran 2 has more stories of fairy encounters. During a wedding at Bennan the whisky ran out, so two men went to the nearest inn for supplies. On the way back a hole opened in the ground and they saw and heard fairies dancing to music. One man entered but the other ran off and told the wedding party what he had seen. Everyone went to the spot, but the hole had disappeared – and the survivor was suspected of murder. The friends of the missing man went to a 'woman of skill', who told them to not to touch the suspected man for a year and a day, and then return to the spot. On the appointed night the hole opened and they saw their friend, still dancing with the jar of whisky on his back. He thought he had been there for just one reel. The people of 'a certain township at the south end of Arran' broke up an old disused burial place so they could feed cattle on the grass there. The site was supposedly guarded by the fairies. When stopping for dinner one of the farmers said, 'surely the little folks think very little of our work since they don't think it worth their while to give us our dinner.' When getting back to work they found a table spread with food. None of them tried it and the fairies were so offended that not one blade of grass grew on the site.

East Bennan (aka Craigdhu) chambered cairn★★ (NR99352075) is one of the best-preserved cairns on the island. There are a number of sizeable stones which mark the façade at the west end, and the large main chamber is visible, as are three other smaller chambers. Bryce excavated the chamber in 1909, but it had been cleared out some time previously, and the only finds were a pitchstone flake and a fragment of a round-bottomed bowl-like vessel, both now lost. The access is the Belagra Farm road, 500yds (460m) east of the track to West Bennan farm. After about 500yds (460m) you come to a field. Bear left (south east) and downhill through a field for about 400yds (365m). (There may well be livestock in the field.)

Hugh McKerrell, in *Isle of Arran – Walking the Past,* claims that another chapel, Kilbride Bennan, once stood about 875yds (800m) south of Kilbride farm. There are no records of this chapel, but McKerrell notes that a Mr Bunty Swan from Catacol recalled that in the 1920s the Kilmory minister the Revd Wright used to ride his horse down here to the site to hold a short service for the people interred there, so presumably there had been burials within living memory.

KILMORY

A short minor road leads north from Kilmory village to the parish church* (NR96332185), erected in 1785 on the site of an earlier building and completely renovated in 1881. The attractive graveyard has gravestones with occupation-specific carvings, such as two sheep for a farmer and a broken anchor for a ship's captain. The most unusual headstone is the white-painted restored figurehead from the *Bessie Arnold*, wrecked off the notorious south shore in a blizzard on 28 December 1908. The wreck was spotted early in the morning, but heavy snow prevented the Kildonan rocket team from arriving for several hours. The Campbeltown lifeboat arrived at 2 p.m., but the seas were so rough – at one point the lifeboat was flung right over the stricken vessel – that it had to withdraw, having only managed to rescue one sailor, the bowman. The rest of the four crew succumbed to the cold and their bodies were eventually washed ashore.

Being the mother-church of over half of the entire island, Kilmory was where kirk-discipline was carried out. Usually this involved handing down punishments for sexual activity or non-attendance at church, but occasionally the kirk session found itself dealing with magic. On 13 June 1708 two Kilmory women, Janet McIlpatrick and Effie McKallan, were said to have stayed away from church in order to make a counter charm against the witchcraft-induced heart disease afflicting Margaret Taylor. They melted down a piece of lead, poured it through a sieve into water and formed it into the shape of a heart. They then told Margaret to keep the amulet on her neck, saying that it would ease her pain. There are no further details of what transpired.

The case is reported in *The Book of Arran 2*, which also describes the tale of Ferguhar Ferguson. On 9 December 1716 Ferguhar was cited and called at the church door and accused of curing people who were elf-shot – that is, suffering pain from small arrowheads fired into them by the fairies. He confessed that he was hired to 'search for holes in people that were suspected to be shot'. The cure – which cost a shilling – was a little black soap and a potion made of the herb agrimony. A voice told him in his sleep that when harvesting the agrimony he must do so in the name of the Father, Son and Holy Ghost, else the cure would not be effective. Ferguhar had acquired his skill a year before when – observing people on the mainland looking for elf-shot holes in sick people and cattle – he was prompted to do the same for his own sick child. Another part of the charge claimed he also used charms, although Ferguhar denied this. There are no details of what the 'charms' might be. The kirk session couldn't decide what to do and referred the case to the Presbytery. As is often the case, there are no further details.

The Book of Arran also gives an example, from 25 October 1705, of the terrifying 'oath of purgation', which would be sworn at the church by those seeking to demonstrate they were telling the truth:

If I lye in this matter or do not speake truth, then I wish and pray with my whole soul that God may confound me with some visible judgment or other, that I may never prosper or thrive in this world, but that all my goods and geir [money] may suddenly vanish and perish and that I may be a beggar and a vagabond and stricken with some loathsome distemper or disease till death seize me and that I may forever be banished from God and the society of the blessed and holy Angels and Saints, and shut up with Devils in the eternal torments of Hell for ever and ever.

In a God-fearing Satan-believing society this was a mighty oath indeed.

The track running north from near the church is signposted to the craft centre at Cloined, site of a fairy abduction reported in *The Book of Arran 2*. The local women were sitting at night with the farmer's wife during her childbirth when there was a terrible roar in the byre as if the cattle were being gored to death. The women went to investigate. The animals were fine – but on their return the wife was gone. One day later the farmer, whose name was Cook, was working at the mouth of the Sliddery Water when he saw a flight of fairies overhead. He threw the reaping hook into the air and his wife immediately appeared next to him. She also told him the fairies were good to her, and that when sweeping the kiln he should leave some grains so the fairies could eat them. She said:

My dear husband, it is not in my power to go with you, but if you leave the front door and back door of the house open on a certain night, I and a company of the little folk will enter between the two doors. Be you sitting waiting, and when you see an opportunity you will throw my wedding-cloak over me and I shall be restored to you.

But when the time came he lost courage and did not throw the cloak over her, and she was never seen again. James Napier, in his 1879 book *Folk Lore, or Superstitious Beliefs in the West of Scotland Within This Century* tells a variant of the same story, from a publication called *Long Ago*. After the woman's abduction:

On a certain night her wraith stood before her husband telling him that the yearly riding was at hand, and that she, with all the rout, should ride by his house at such an hour, on such a night; that he must await her coming, and throw over her the gown from her wedding day, and so she should be rescued from her tyrants. With that she vanished. And the time came, with the jingling of bridles and the tramping of horses outside the cottage; but this man, feeble-hearted, had summoned his neighbours to bear him company, who held him, and would not suffer him to go out. So there arose a bitter cry and a great clamor, and then all was still; but in the morning, roof and wall were dashed with blood, and the sorrowful wife was no more seen upon earth.

'This,' says the writer, 'is not a tale from an old ballad, it is the narrative of what was told not fifty years ago.' *The Book of Arran 2* also relates the episode of a woman from Claynod (Cloined) who, on her way home from visiting a sick person, met a headless man. She recognized him as a man who had died some months ago. Such was her shock that she died the following day.

The track past Cloined is the starting point for the long trek to Aucheleffan Stone Circle (aka Allt Nan Tighean) and Carn Ban Chambered Cairn. After a slow, straight climb through forestry, pass through Aucheleffan farm and then go left (west) at the next junction. The stone circle is a further mile (1km) on, in a small clearing on the left (NR97842505). Stone circle doyenne Aubrey Burl, in *A Guide to the Stone Circles of Britain, Ireland and Brittany* describes Aucheleffan as a 'perfect four-poster'. The four granite stones, arranged in a square, are a maximum of 3ft 6ins (1m) high. The site was excavated in 1903, but nothing was found. It is a fine place for a picnic, and you'll probably deserve the rest, although the view was better some years ago – *The Book of Arran 2* has a photograph of the circle on a completely bare moorland, not a conifer in sight.

To get to Carn Ban, retrace your steps to the track junction, then go left (east). After about 1¼ miles (2km) you meet the mountain bike trail. Turn left (north) then take the next fork left (east), signposted Carn Ban. The Clyde group chambered long cairn is in a clearing surrounded by dense forestry at NR99192620. Historic Scotland have taken Carn Ban into state care because it is an important type-site, but unfortunately in its current state it is hard to get excited about it, especially if you've just trekked for miles uphill through rather dull forestry plantations to get there. The cairn is large, and with a bit of study you can make out the long body, and at the north-east, the semicircular façade of stones which fronted onto the forecourt. The chamber is not visible as it was filled in after the excavation of 1903. Overall, it's a bit dismal. 'Canmore', the RCAHMS website, mentions a nineteenth-century report stating that there was a circle of low stones 40ft (12m) in diameter in front of the cairn. The few finds – a flint flake, a pitch-stone flake, and a fragment of human bone – along with a flint scraper and a box of flakes and chips found nearby in 1969, are in the National Museum of Scotland.

An alternative, signposted mountain bike route leaves the A841 at NR970214, east of Kilmory. After passing Auchareoch on the left, take the next left, then two rights, to Aucheleffan. Return the same way to the cycle route, turn left (north) and follow the directions above to Carn Ban. If you take the cycleway to the end you pass Meallach's Grave chambered cairn (see THE ROSS).

LAGG

For the footsore or soaked, relief and good food can be found here at both the tea-room and the eighteenth-century Lagg Inn. The latter is reputedly haunted by a local laird who sold his soul to the Devil in return for sufficient cash to clear his debts. Other ghosts – this time the spirits of two young lovers who were mistaken for smugglers and shot by coastguards – supposedly lurk in the woods above the village. Cnoc a' Chrochaidh, to the north at NR953227, translates as the Hill of the Hanging, but I can find no tradition linked to it.

TORRYLINN★

Also known as Torlin, this chambered cairn is much easier – and much more enjoyable – to visit than Carn Ban. Several short paths lead here through the woods from the post office and the community hall in Lagg (the latter has better parking). Following the path further takes you to the beach. The site (NR955211) is in the care of Historic Scotland and has good interpretation; you may find the manicured neatness of the setting contrasts with the sheer ruin of the monument. The chamber is open and obvious. The largest remaining stone on the site contains what may be fossil shells.

John McArthur, in his 1861 book *The Antiquities of Arran*, relays some of the traditions surrounding this site. The chambers of the cairn were apparently:

> Filled with human bones, some of which, we were informed, were cleft as if from the blow of an axe or hatchet. This cairn was partially removed some years ago by a modern Goth, who rifled the cells of their contents, and strewed them over his field. With daring irreverence, he selected one of the largest skulls from the ghastly heap, and carried it home with him; but scarcely had he entered his house when its walls were shaken as if struck by a tornado. Again and again the avenging blast swept over his dwelling, though not a sigh of the gentlest breeze was heard in the neighbouring wood. The affrighted victim hastened to re-bury the bones in their desecrated grave, but day and night shadowy phantoms continued to haunt his mind and track his steps, and a few months after the commission of his rash deed, whilst riding along the high road towards Lag, he was thrown from his horse over a steep embankment, and dashed against the rocks of the stream beneath. This tradition is well known in Arran, and has tended to deepen the feelings of superstitious dread with which these monuments are generally regarded.

McArthur excavated 'this ghost-haunted cairn' but only found a few marine shells and bird bones. Further excavations in 1900 by Thomas Bryce found that the fourth compartment in the chamber had been overlooked by both the antiquarians and the grave-robbers, and contained the bones of six adults, a child and an infant, 'scattered in great confusion... embedded in a black soil, compressed into an almost stony hardness' (*The Book of Arran 1*). Also discovered were the bones of adult ox, pig, fox, dog and otter, as well as piglet and lamb or kid, and part of a bowl and a flint scraper.

CLACHAIG

½mile (800m) west of Lagg a track marked 'Cart Track Cleats Shore' runs south. Looking east from the track you can see the conspicuous 'Ossian's Mound', one of the many places in Scotland where the mythical Fingalian is supposed to be buried. The barrow is south of Clachaig Farm (NR95022143). *The Name Book* of 1864 records that a Mr Spiers dug into the tumulus to erect a flagstaff, and encountered a stone-lined cist containing human bones. An excavation in 1900 located a second cist, but both graves were empty apart from a piece of pottery and a flake of flint. Several large stones can be seen on the top, but there is no obvious trace of the cists. Note that this is not a chambered cairn but two separate burials dug into a large mound. To reach Clachaig Chambered Cairn (NR94932118) continue along the track and after the gate and before the cliff turn left (east) through the field, cross the stream and head up the slope. There is not much to see here, the cairn being damaged and robbed to build the limekiln to the south, and the stones of the chamber barely visible. The cairn dates to around 3500BC, in the Neolithic. In 1900 Bryce found bones from fourteen people, a stone axe and two Neolithic bowls (a replica of one of the bowls is in Brodick Castle); a secondary short cist yielded bone fragments and an urn and flint knife. The National Museum of Scotland in Edinburgh has the artifacts while the bones lie in the Hunterian Museum, Glasgow. One of the skulls was used as the basis for the reconstruction of the face of 'Clachaig Man', now in the ARRAN HERITAGE MUSEUM. In the 1980s the beach at Cleats Shore was designated, somewhat optimisticall, as a naturist beach.

BENNECARRIGAN & SLIDDERY

Once a horse was bewitched. A Bennecarrigan man, skilled in countercharms, made a mixture of soot, salt and water and poured it into a bottle, emphatically warning the messenger not to take the cork out on the way – but she took a swig before sprinkling it on the animal. When there was no effect the man was summoned and stated the original liquid must have been tampered with. He created a new potion on the spot, passed it nine times around his head and then poured a few drops in the horse's ears and threw the residue into the fire. In a few minutes the horse was quite well. The tale is in *The Book of Arran 2*.

Just east of where the Sliddery Water meets the beach is a small hillock, Cnocan Ceusaidh, supposedly 'the hill of torture' (NR935221). Traditionally this is where a large number of plague victims were interred. The mound is natural and there is no evidence of burials. On the other side of the Water is Kelpie Cottage. I have no information on why it is named after a malevolent supernatural aquatic creature – unless it is somehow linked to the House of the Monster (see below).

About 400yds (365m) north from Sliddery Bridge, on the east side of Sliddery Water (NR93992301), is the site of St Mary's Chapel, the original medieval parish church before it was transferred to the present site at KILMORY. In a clear act of folk magic drawing on the power of the consecrated ground, the earth of the old churchyard was taken and strewn over the new burial ground. *The New Statistical Account* of 1845 refers to a 'beautifully carved' stone here, but this, along with the entire church and graveyard, has disappeared. As late as 1864 the site was still sufficiently venerated for it to be used as an occasional burial ground for infants, although by the same year the miraculous healing well somewhere nearby had been ploughed over. In his 1937 manuscript 'Postman's Journey', Corriecravie man Donald Stewart calls it 'the ancient well of St Molios where the McKinnons draw their water'. A spot below on Sliddery Water was called the Churchyard Pool.

The ghost of a little girl in distress is supposedly seen near the former mill building on the north side of the main road near here. The story is that she was run down and killed by a horse and cart, or by a coach and horses.

There are several folkloric and archaeological sites on the moors north of Bennecarrigan/Sliddery. Because Sliddery Water is a considerable barrier, I have listed here only those sites west of the Water which can be reached on foot from Sliddery. For the sites which can only really be accessed from THE ROSS minor road, please see that chapter.

The Allt na Pairce, the first western tributary of the Sliddery Water, forms a small tree-shrouded valley going north-west. Somewhere between 200 and 300yds (180–275m) up the small burn was Tigh-na-Bhieta – according to Donald Stewart's memoir, 'a place much dreaded by the old folks of by-gone generations – the name means the Evil One or Spirit.' *The Book of Arran 2* calls it Tigh na Beisd, the House of the Monster, saying: 'There are huge flagstones strewn about, said to have been used in the building of the female giant's house'. It is impossible to identify any of this now.

Further north, and atop a slope west of Sliddery Water, is Oscar's Grave chambered cairn (NR94272374). Oscar was another mythical Fingalian hero, the warrior son of Ossian (who is himself supposedly buried at Ossian's Mound at CLACHAIG). Currie's *The Place-Names of Arran* gives two possible derivations for the name 'Sliddery' – *Slidhr*, from the Norse, 'place of swords', or *Slaodrie*, Gaelic, 'place of slaughter'. There is a long tradition of a battle in the area – either between the Fingalians and the Vikings, or a more local derby. McArthur (*The Antiquities of Arran*) notes that nearby at Margareach there was a stone column marking a peace treaty between the islanders and the Norsemen, while Headrick gives Margareach as the site of a tumulus where many heroes were buried after a battle. For an encounter with the unquiet ghosts of the warriors, see THE ROSS. The nineteenth-century descriptions of Oscar's Grave call it a ship-shaped cairn with a large standing stone at each end. Sadly its glory days are gone. The site had been rifled long before the excavation of 1901 – McArthur describes 'an anxious treasure-seeker' who was said 'to have found a huge bone, into the hollow of which he thrust down his foot and leg as into a boot' – and it's something of a disappointment.

Archaeologists have identified a late Neolithic/early Bronze Age tool working area high on the moor above the Allt-na-Pairce burn at NR935242. Flint and pitchstone scrapers, arrowheads, blades, knives, perforators, cores, core scrapers and chisels have been found, along with pottery, a stone axe, a copper alloy ring and four curious small wooden wheel and roller-like objects.

CORRIECRAVIE

The people of Arran still regard the old fortlet with a superstitious dread, and he is thought to have a bold heart who will venture to disturb its ruins or visit them after nightfall. (John McArthur *The Antiquities of Arran*, 1861)

McArthur's 'old fortlet' is Torr a' Chaisteil★ (NR92192326), a ruined grass-covered Iron Age dun atop a conspicuous mound. The site is in the care of Historic Scotland. The mound appears artificial but is actually an old headland, now some distance from the sea. The dun itself, a small fortified dwelling, dates from roughly AD 100-200. Access is via a signposted path south from the road, via a stile and a kissing gate, and then for 550yd (500m) following the edge of a field. Note that a sign says 'no dogs' – there are sheep in the field – and there is nowhere to park at the start of the path, the nearest parking being in Sliddery, mile (1km) to the east. The circular wall of the fortification is now quite hard to make out. The most distinctive feature is the number of parallel ridges snaking around the mound. McArthur says these were known as elf-furrows.

Perhaps related to this is the story of an eighteenth-century folk healer from Corriecravie called 'Doctor' McLarty. *The Book of Arran 2* tells how on the first day he went to school he was met by a little green-coated man who took him to a fairy college underneath Torr a' Chaisteil, and there secretly educated him in the healing arts. He also learned the 'skill of rebuking' from the 'big old wife of Torlin', presumably an older woman skilled in such things. Another tale in *The Book of Arran 2* reveals something of the ambivalent way the 'doctor' was viewed. A long time ago the son of a gauger (an exciseman) in Lochranza was profoundly ill. The local wise woman could do not anything for him, so the only course of action was to go up the magical-healing hierarchy and send for McLarty, also known as the Doctor Bàn. A young lad was despatched on the gauger's own yellow mare. At Tormore he met an old man putting cows to the hill and explained his mission. The old man gave him some advice: attach a bunch of rowans at the root of your horse's tail, carry a good hazel stick in your fist, and if you feel a weakness of heart or body coming on, say: 'The evil of thine eye be upon thee.' And, most importantly, be sure that the doctor does not get the first sight of the gauger's house, for if he then is successful in his healing mission, you will die in the boy's place. The lad gave thanks, implemented the apotropaic devices, and went on to locate the doctor. Returning to Lochranza, the youth made sure he rode at the front, with the doctor on his grey shaggy pony behind him. When they reached Bealach-an-iomachair (Imachar, south of Whitefarland), the doctor tried to sneak in front, but the lad hit the mare smartly and took the lead again. At Bealach-a-chrò the lad felt his heart getting faint and his body weak. He repeated the words 'The evil of thine eye be upon thee' and felt better. At Catacol the doctor, clearly peeved, said, 'since there is such haste in the matter, and that you have no cause for haste, let us make an exchange of horses.' The lad replied, 'thank you, but my own life is more necessary to myself than the life of another.' He gave another blow to the mare and made sure he arrived first at Lochranza. During the consultation the doctor said to the gauger with anger, 'why did you send for me by one who was as skilful as myself? I cannot do anything for your son.' And the gauger's boy died shortly after.

McArthur further elaborates the fairy nature of Torr a' Chaisteil. The mound was fertile ground, so twelve local families each claimed a rig or farming strip on it. The grass was cleared and cabbages planted. 'But a signal retribution followed the commission of this daring sacrilege. Before the year closed, the children of the hamlet were fatherless, and eleven new graves were seen in the little churchyard of the district.' The one man who escaped had been in another part of the island when the sacrilegious crops were planted, and so avoided the supernatural retribution. When McArthur excavated he found quantities of animal bones and shells, but all the human bones supposedly found on site had presumably been removed in an earlier, unrecorded dig. At the start of the twentieth century a partial excavation turned up bones of pig and deer, the top stone of a quern, and a piece of haematite iron ore, but further investigations were rained off.

Torr a' Chasteil, prehistoric dun and fairy dwelling.

To the north-west where two streams meet at NR92252353 is Sron Liath, once believed
to be a burial place or tumulus, but it is just a natural hummock.

When the Ordnance Survey were in the area in the 1860s three local informants
from Corriecravie pointed out two 'graves' somewhere in the area, linking them to
a great battle supposedly fought here long ago between the islanders and a party
of raiders from Kintyre, with the former victorious. The body of the chief of the
McAlisters was said to be buried in one grave, with his severed head in the other.
The sites were not confirmed as ancient at the time, or even as genuine graves, and
they, and their exact location, are long lost.

The Book of Arran 2 tells several tales of Innis Eabhra, the enchanted island, which
lies under the sea near the Iron Rock off the Corriecravie shore. At times it was so
manifest that corn stooks could be seen in the fields, and women putting clothes out
to dry. It was last seen about 1864 or so, when a farmer saw the island rising near to
the shore. Running closer to get a better view he briefly lost sight of it in a hollow,
and when his sightline returned, the island had vanished. Another day, a stranger leading a grey filly by the halter took passage from Ayr to Arran. When they approached
the Iron Rock the filly began to neigh and other neighs were heard in response
from under the sea. The man asked the crew to throw the horse overboard, and then
jumped after it himself. A year later the skipper met the man at Ayr market. 'I saw you
before now,' said the skipper. 'If you did you will not see another for ever,' replied the
stranger, and struck the skipper with the palm of his hand, leaving him blind – a traditional punishment for those who spot fairies out of their environment, and a story
whose variants are told throughout Scotland. Fisherman waiting to lift their nets
would hear music and song from beneath the waves on calm, still nights:

Where have you left the fair men, Ho ro golaidh u lé?
We left them on the sea-girt isle, Ho ro golaidh u lé.
Back to back with no breath in them, Ho ro golaidh u lé.

A story about a 'mermaid' from Innis Eabhra is an example of the shape-shifting seal-
woman 'selkie' tale common throughout the West Coast and islands. A farmer from
Kilpatrick came across her in human form asleep on the shore, with her magic cloak
by her side. He snatched the cloak, which compelled her to follow him and do his
bidding. They were married and had a son and daughter. Seven years later when he
was at church on Sunday the children found the cloak in the barn and showed it to
their mother. Reunited with her transformative garment she was able to return to the
sea. At times she would come ashore at Rudha 'n-loin to comb her children's hair and
sing them songs. The girl grew up a great beauty and some of her offspring, Sliochd
an Ròin (the brood of the seal), were still alive in 1914. The tale does have an unusual element in that the woman's young son chose to follow her into the ocean and
became transformed into a seal. For a very modern take on the selkie motif, which
may possibly have been inspired by this story, see BLACKWATERFOOT.

There are several enigmatic prehistoric monuments on the lower slopes of Cnoc
Reamhar, north of Corriecravie and south-west of the quarry and the building called
The Moor. None of the sites are marked on the Ordnance Survey map. On the
120m contour (NR927242) is a mound with a chamber, with a large flat stone 50yds
(45m) north-west, which may be the capstone or a lintel. A small cist lies (NR929243)
on a rocky spur, and at roughly the same height (NR929244) is another substantial

chamber, with an arc of three upright stones to the south, and more stones to the north. Other, less obvious, stone settings dot the immediate area. A more accessible cairn stands just to the east of the roadside (NR90572448), and although it is very badly damaged an arc of the former circular kerb can be made out. Find the mile-stone and head south for about 60yds (55m).

The strange straight but up-and-down road running north towards Blackwaterfoot is known as the Leacach Bhreac or the Leac a bhreac and has its share of folklore. One of the stories was related by Corriecravie man Donald Stewart (who also told the story of the farmer Cook and his fairy-abducted wife in Cloined near KILMORY) in an address to the Arran Ceilidh in 1924:

> The Leac a bhreac was always associated with Bochans… a good old man of Bennicarrigan of the name of Cook, a weaver to trade, had been weaving a web of cloth at Shiskine, and was delayed there until it was late when he started out to wend his homeward way through the Leac a breac, and had just passed Cnoc an Avack when he became aware of something walking alongside of him, and on looking round fearfully to see what it was that accompanied him, he saw the form of a big black dog, with red glowing eyes, keeping step for step with him, which it did until past Ces an tram Bheiredh. Then it began to speak to him and it told him that if it was not for that darning needle he had in his cap, it would tell him where a great ooly or treasure was hidden. However he got the strength to say to it: 'Get thee gone, Satan!' And it left him and went over the cliff with a noise as if tons of chains were falling over… I have known grown women who did not care to come through the Leac a bhreac even in the day time.

(For another tale of a steel darning needle, an ooly and a thwarted evil spirit, see MACHRIE MOOR and THE STRING.)

Another story is told in *The Book of Arran 2* is of a Kilpatrick farmer who went to Leacach Bhreac to cut brackens. Suddenly the sky darkened and something like a swarm of bees obscured the sun. He threw his reaping hook into the air – as you do – and his wife, supposedly ill in bed, fell on him. He took her home and threw her into a chaff corner in the barn, and went into the house. There he found a black ugly old woman in bed, shivering. He asked after her condition and she replied she was indeed very cold. So he built up the fire to a great height. When it was burning well he picked the old woman up and threw her on the blaze. She let out a terrible scream and went up the chimney. The farmer then took a rope and thrashed his wife thoroughly until she promised never to go on a similar aerial journey again. This tale seems to mix fairy and witchcraft motifs.

More fairy activity is associated with the curious structure at NR90192565, just east of the road (called 'Stones' on the OS 1:25000 map). According to *The Book of Arran 2* it was known as the Fairy's Bed, wherein the local people prepared a cot for the annual visit of a good fairy. If he came and occupied the bed, all was well. If not, bad luck followed. The site is described as three stones – two opposite each other, the third at right angles – with five more stones just to the south, although just what this site is cannot be established. Unfortunately there are hundreds of granite boulders and slabs scattered across the bracken- and heather-covered slope here, and after tramping over the hillside for an hour in the pouring rain without finding the Fairy's Bed, I was forced to admit defeat. Perhaps you'll have better luck.

7

THE WEST COAST

KILPATRICK

Several sites on Arran have puzzled archaeologists, and the Historic Scotland monument here (NR90652619) is one of them. The confusion starts with the signposting: at the car park it is labeled 'Cashel' (a Dark Ages monastic site), while the interpretation panel on the site talks of a 'dun' (a fortified Iron Age farm or settlement occupied by a single family). And neither mention the possible Neolithic and Bronze Age origins of the site. As you approach the farm from the car park take the first track to the right (not the track from the main farm area). Keep the burn on your left. St Patrick's Chapel once stood on the site of the farm (NR90322685). In the nineteenth century one corner of the area remained undisturbed because it was basically a bone field. The route runs south-east uphill for about ½mile (800-900m) and although there are frequent directional pointers, at the crucial point – when you are faced with a fork in the track – the arrows disappear. Take the less-used path to the left – you should be able to see the next pointer in the distance on the ridge above. The site itself is a large enclosure surrounded by an earth and stone bank, with a substantial circular stone structure in the north wall.

Balfour, who excavated it in the early twentieth century, was very excited by this extensive monument, interpreting it as a cashel, a group of cells for Irish-Celtic monks, possibly founded by St Brandon in the sixth century. Brandon gave his name to Kilbrannon Sound, between Arran and Kintyre. In later years a semi-fortified monastery was thought to have been built on this early holy site. *The Book of Arran 1* describes how bodies were supposedly brought from Ireland specifically to be buried at Kilpatrick. Temporary burial was given until there were sufficient dead for a shipment. The process was stopped after a corpse ship sank in the Irish Channel. 'Part of the tradition was that the bodies were always carried over running water before being buried.' Unfortunately for this romantic, sub-Iona 'island of the dead' story, there was never any archaeological evidence for the cashel, and this may be a case of wish-fulfillment based on little more than the name, derived from St Patrick, and the superficial resemblance between the ground plan of the site and known cashels in Ireland.

A more realistic modern assessment has concluded the site is actually earlier, the circular structure being the remains of a dun, a defended farmstead, possibly dating from around AD200. The extensive bank is seen as an enclosure for crops or animals, part of a dispersed prehistoric farming settlement. In low sunlight rig and furrows marks can be made out. The bank has a number of small rectangular stone structures, once thought to be part of the monastery, now interpreted as bothies. Now the story gets complicated: in 1909 Balfour found a short cist beneath the wall of the homestead, containing a Bronze Age urn. Other investigations suggest a complex of Bronze Age burial cists may underlie the structure of the dun. And some of the larger stones may even be from a Neolithic chambered tomb. The turf bank also incorporates the occasional large stone, which looks suspiciously grandiose. It all suggests the site was originally a Neolithic, and then a Bronze Age, cemetery, which was reused for agricultural purposes in the Iron Age. But definitely not an Irish monastic site.

Across the burn just to the east are four hut circles, with two more 380yds (347m) to the west. All of them were once identified as monastic cells. The immediate area has the occasional cairn – which may be clearance or funereal – and the odd suggestive boulder. A definite, but much damaged, cist is in the forestry to the south-east (NR908526og) mile (1km) to the north-east, just inside the boundary of the forest, is the equally demolished Carmahome Chambered Cairn (NR9149200o). This site is of exceptional archaeological interest however, because, unlike all the other chambered cairns on Arran, which are 'Clyde'-type with chambers of successive galleries, Carmahome is a passage-grave, in which a passage leads from the outside into a single central chamber. As such it has more in common with the 'Clava'-style cairns found around Inverness and the north of Scotland. Could it represent an exotic ritual practice that somehow never caught on in Arran?

Opposite the parking area for the cashel a walk signposted 'footpath' leads west from the road, then about 220yds (200m) south along the other side of a fence to the Preaching Cave★ (NR900267). Note that there are three caves in the cliffs here – the Preaching Cave is the one in the middle and can be identified by it having a substantial path to its entrance, the junction with the main path being marked by a large boulder. The cave was used for Christian worship from at least the seventeenth to the nineteenth centuries, and also saw use as a school, taught by Peter Craig. Until a new Free Church was built, services – sometimes lasting for almost four hours – were regularly heard here during the 1843 Disruption in the Church of Scotland. *The Book of Arran 2* tells of two brothers who were on the way to a service. One pointed to the rocks on the shore and asked: 'Did you see that?' but his brother saw nothing. The first man told the other to put one foot on his own and to look again. This was common practice for the physical transfer of second sight in Scotland, and this time the second man did indeed see the wraith – which was of his brother. The man who had seen his own wraith died in the Preaching Cave.

Archaeologically the cave is a virtually a nul-zone, the only artefact found having been a bone sewing awl. The cave is high-roofed with a flat floor and, as long as the wind or rain is not coming directly in, it is probably one of the most comfortable caves on Arran, a situation perhaps confirmed by the extensive evidence of campfires, and the exuberant quality of the modern graffiti. In January 2008 there was a wooden board lodged at the end of the cave with the following inscription: 'Gary 'n' Isabell Fulton. Five years married today 26th Jan 2006… spent the day here in this cave. Will be back next year.' And then a coda: 'Came back 30th Jan 07.' Good on you Gary 'n' Isabell. The former religious use of the cave was perhaps reflected in another item present at the time, a memorial wreath to a local man who had died in 1997.

South of the A841/B880 junction a short minor road runs to the east, to Achavoulin, Bailemargaidh and Druimaghineir. Archie Craig – who for two decades came to the school every year to share his memories and the old stories with the children – told this tale to Alison Murchie of Bailemargaidh in 1984. Bailemargaidh means market place or village, and nearby can still be seen Clach an Fheoladair, the Flesher's Stone or Auctioneer's Stone, where people bartered goods (NR905277). One market day a boy was sent to the beach to watch for raiders. He nodded off, coming to just as a party of ne'er-do-wells from Campbeltown were coming up the beach. The boy ran to the fair to give warning, but was out of breath when he arrived, and before his stuttering could be understood the raiders were upon them. The burn here is Allt Gille Ghagaich, burn of the stuttering boy. In the battle Laidir Mhari, Strong Mary, was knocked unconscious and carried off on a raider's shoulder. She recovered, throttled the man, then laid him out with the club that had been used on her. She carried him back to Bailemargaidh and after a while they got married and lived happily ever after. Archie Craig died in 2000, aged ninety. His story can be found in the Arran Heritage Community Group's book *Isle of Arran Heritage*.

In 1895 a seventy-nine-year-old crofter from Druimaghineir related a story to Alexander Carmichael of a local farmer called Macuga or Cook who took a trip to Ireland with the fairies. Carmichael included it in his monumental study of Gaelic folklore, *Carmina Gadelica*. Essentially the same story, but with much more detail, and the name of the fellow traveller given as MacMurchie, is also told in *The Book of Arran 2*. Fairies lived near Druimaghineir in the knoll of Cnoc 'ic Eoghain (possibly Cnocan Donn, NR918279) and MacMurchie the farmer often visited them there, always putting a knife, darning needle or other metal in the doorway to ensure an exit. One night the fairies congregated on the top of the hillock. Each pulled a ragwort, said some mystic words and stood astride the plant. One fairy asked if they were all ready, and when the host replied that they were, the flight controller called out, 'My king at my head, going across in my haste, on the crests of the waves, to Ireland.' 'Follow me,' said the King of the fairies, and away they were across the Irish ocean. MacMurchie repeated the action and followed them over the Mull of Kintyre to Ireland. Soon he was in the kitchen of a farmer, where the housewife was in her deathbed. The fairies snatched her away and left in her place a 'stock' – a log with her appearance. They returned to Arran and, because he had accompanied them, bestowed the woman on MacMurchie. She duly became his wife. Seven years later on a warm summer evening an Irish beggar sat down on the husking-stone at the side of MacMurchie's door. He saw the woman and said, 'Well, if I had not placed my wife with my own two hands in the coffin, I would swear that thou art she.' It was of course her original husband and in the end she left with him. I think modern soap operas could do with using more of this kind of storyline.

The above story is in *The Book of Arran 2*, as is an episode which took place around about 1838. A Druimaghiner man was returning home with a cartload of seaweed when he was approached by a fellow who tried to buy his mare from him. The farmer refused to sell, and as soon as the man left, the horse became ill. He was forced to unyoke her as she was white with foam, and had kicked her shoes clean off. The farmer sent for Hugh McKenzie, a famous curer. As soon as he saw the horse Hugh knew who had done it. He obtained salt and soot and added some secret ingredients he had with him, made a ball, and gave part to the mare. The rest he threw into the fire where it exploded noisily. In a few minutes the horse recovered.

FEORLINE

In 1845 a wall of the thatched school building collapsed, killing five young girls. It had been loosened by frost and thaw. A few days earlier a girl called Mysie Bannatyne had been on her way home when she saw five small coffins placed on the parapet of the bridge beside the classroom. When she got to her father's house she collapsed from fright. After the catastrophe the bodies of the girls were indeed laid on the bridge. The story was related in 1983 by pupil Kirsteen Pringle and recorded in *Isle of Arran Heritage*.

The Book of Arran 2 describes an eye-witness account of the unbewitching of a cow at Feorline in the 1850s. Soot was swept down from the chimney into an ashtray made of calfskin stretched on a hoop like the side of a drum. The soot was mixed with salt and made into three little balls which were placed inside a blade of kail and fed to the cow. Then salt was put into a bowl of water with a gold ring and a sixpenny piece (sometimes a piece of coal was used as well). The water stirred and sprinkled on the cow in the form of the cross from head to tail. Some of the water was poured in the animal's ears and – after taking out the coin and ring – the remainder was thrown onto the cinders at the back of the fireplace. During all this the cureperson would repeat a Gaelic rhyme meaning something like, 'If they have eaten you, let them spew you.' A similar ceremony – minus the eating of the salt/soot mixture – was seen by the witness on the mainland in Ayr in the 1870s, performed by a Shiskine woman upon a young bride who was unwell.

According to *The Book of Arran 2*, the Curries of Tigh-Meadhonach (now Tighenmenach, South Feorline) had a pact with a fairy. As long as water was not spilled at the back door of the farm and its people were under her protection, and she crooned in Gaelic, 'Holy are the children! Holy are the children! The housewife knows I am not a witch.' But the Curries left the farm and the Crawfords took their place. They did not know the fairy's secret and spilled water at the back door – and everything went wrong. The children screamed, the porridge singed, soot came down the chimney. Eventually the Crawfords left, the Curries returned and domestic harmony was restored.

SHISKINE

The attractive Victorian St Molio's church on the east side of the road at Birchburn (NR90992941) has a superb full-length carved figure* built into the south-west angle of the tower. The effigy is tonsured and has vestments, a chalice and staff. It was originally sited at the graveyard in PIEN, where until the late-eighteenth century women who had given birth would leave a silver coin on the stone as thanks for their recovery. The stone was moved in 1889. The reverence attached to the stone derives from the belief that it represents St Molios (see HOLY ISLAND for the full St Molios story). There was also a holy well named after Molios somewhere nearby (in 1937 Corriecravie postman Donald Stewart identified its location as being near SLIDDERY). Thomas Pennant, in his 1772 *Tour to the Hebrides* says, 'in Shiskin or Seasgain churchyard is a tomb called that of Maol-Jos, that is, "The servant of Jesus"... The stone was broken about half a year ago by some sacrilegious fellow in search of treasure... the attempt did not go unpunished as soon afterwards, the audacious wretch was visited with a broken leg.' Pennant is responsible for the erroneous identification of Molios with St Molaise of HOLY ISLAND (for which see for the full, complicated story).

Briefly, Molaise was an early Christian saint active on Holy Island in the late sixth century, while Molios, who is otherwise undocumented, may have had his base at

Shiskine much later, in the Middle Ages. Folk memory – possibly aided by the likes of Pennant's factitious account and its effect on later high-status travellers – confused the two because of the similarity of names. Some eighteenth-century evidence – such as the healing charm recorded during a kirk session discipline case at KILBRIDE in LAMLASH – makes it clear that Molaise and Molios were regarded as two different people. There are problems with a positive identification, however, as Molios does not appear in any contemporary records, and 'Molios' can be a generic name for any monk.

The alleged 'St Molios' effigy, more probably a thirteenth-century cleric, at Shiskine church.

Entwined monsters on the drainpipe.

There is a tradition that the stone was brought from Iona, but this cannot be the case. Steer and Bannerman in their authoritative *Late Medieval Sculpture in the West Highlands* note that the style is stiffer than the later schools of West Highland carving and correspondingly date it to the thirteenth century. They also suggest that since the Cistercian abbey at Saddell (on the mainland in Kintyre, to the west) owned land at Shiskine, the carving may be that of an elderly abbot who retired there. Equally it may be St Benedict (whose writings inspired the foundation of the Cistercian Order) or the patron saint of the church. So we have a carving in the style of a medieval ecclesiastic which may represent an early saint, or a real abbot, or a real-life churchman who may or not have been called St Molios, or may be an entirely unknown, or may have had the name St Molios attached to it at a later date for reasons we will never know. Entwined monsters are carved on the water collectors above the carving.

PIEN

An unmarked track just north of the bridge leads east to the ruined chapel and the burial ground★ (NR92163034). The graveyard supposedly holds the grave of St Molios (see HOLY ISLAND) and was the original location for the carved effigy at SHISKINE, which once lay in the centre. As such the site was highly revered and McArthur says coffins were carried over the hills from Lamlash for burial here. In 1832 there were still the remains of one or two elaborate floral crosses here, and although they are long gone the graveyard is still worth visiting. Immediately to the west is the roofless ruined chapel★, built in 1805 on the site of an earlier church from

Pien old graveyard – horseshoe at the entrance.

around 1708, itself probably on the site of the small medieval chapel dedicated to St Molios. The place was known as Clachan or Clauchan and many of the older records use this name.

The New Statistical Account of 1845 includes an extract from the kirk records of Kilmory, relating to a session held at Clachan on 4 September 1709. Janet Hunter was questioned about an act of divination, the turning of the riddle [sieve] to discover a theft. She confessed to doing it on behalf of Barbara McMarchie and said Florence McDonald, servant to Hector McAlister, assisted her. Janet would repeatedly say, 'by Peter, by Paul, it was such a person,' and the riddle turned at one particular name, indicating the thief. When asked who turned the riddle, she said she did not know, but it was not her or Florence. The interrogator suggested it was therefore either God or Satan. And it certainly wasn't the Almighty. Janet was ordered to 'make her compearance before the congregation three several Sabbaths, to give evidence of her repentance' and was also referred to the civil magistrate to be punished as he saw fit.

The Book of Arran 2 records a number of cases of the supernatural in Shiskine. The last person in the district who made use of a twig of mountain ash to protect his cows from witchcraft was James McA——, a cottar, who died around 1874. He used red string to tie it to their tails. A sprig of rowan was also placed above the byre door. Sometime between the 1860s and the 1890s an apotropaic ritual took place at Tigh-an-Fhraoich, in which some quicksilver was placed inside a hollow stick and the stick placed under one of the flagstones in the byre. About 1894 a man who was bedridden for a long time with a badly sprained leg believed he was bewitched. Conventional medicine was ineffective so he secretly asked John McAlister, a man known for curing elf-shots in cattle, to work on him. After the ritual he unfortunately could not say if he was better or worse.

A man in Shisken was once sowing corn. When taking his rest he saw a small beetle purposefully removing seeds of corn from his field and depositing them on to his neighbour's land. This was obviously witchcraft in action so he captured the insect in his snuffbox. For several days thereafter his neighbour's wife was mysteriously absent. When he finally opened the snuffbox, out she sprang, fully human. (This is a motif found throughout the West of Scotland; sometimes the magical creature is a tiny mouse.)

BALMICHAEL/BALLYMICHAEL

One day, while reaping, an old midwife from Balmichael came across a large ugly frog heavy with young. 'I pray and beseech you that you will not part with your burden until my two hands be about you,' she said, touching and moving the frog out of the way with the sickle. A night or two later a young man came and summoned her and on horseback they went, not out on the road but up to the height of Ard Bheinn (NR945328), where they entered a cave which led into an unearthly great room. The youth told her to take neither food nor drink nor hire, or else she would be like him, 'under the dripping of the torches, without the power to return to house or family.' The frog had been the queen of the fairies in raniform disguise. Having been touched by iron when the prayer had been uttered, she could not give birth until the midwife came and broke the spell. A son was duly delivered and after he was washed and clothed the fairies gave the woman an ointment with which to anoint his eyes.

When she absent-mindedly scratched her eyebrow with the ointmented finger, the midwife found that one eye saw the room as luxurious and grand, while the other saw only a filthy cave. Heeding the messenger's warning, she refused all food and drink, and with her new vision could see that the gold she was offered was in fact horse dung. Eventually she was set back on the horse and she recognised the rider as her neighbour's son, who was thought to have died. At cock crow they arrived at her house and both youth and horse vanished forever. The episode is in *The Book of Arran 2*. For more frog fairies see LOCHRANZA.

A scatter of prehistoric sites are located over an area centred on the outdoor activity visitor centre. In the peat and heather to the north, and west of the water works, is a triangle of stones, probably the remains of a four-poster stone circle (NR92443225). Further to the north-west at NR91903253 are two stones, again the probable wreck of a four-stone circle. Although neither of these sites are amazingly impressive their lonely and little-visited setting gives them a certain aura.

Carrying on further west over the boggy moor brings you to the stone circle complex at MACHRIE MOOR. East of the road at NR92623103 is a strikingly large but fallen standing stone called Uaigh Fiannach, the heroic grave, supposedly the resting place of one of the Fingalian heroes. A little to the north, at NR92723119, a prominent knoll houses what might be an extremely damaged chambered cairn. An urn and flint arrowheads turned up in the nineteenth century. To the south are the remains of a corn-drying kiln. And on the north side of Ballymichael Glen, east of the road, are four obvious hut circles (NR93053180). For sites further up the road, see the chapter on THE STRING.

BLACKWATERFOOT

The village nestles around a tiny harbour and is a good base for exploring the south and west. A number of the older houses and walls were built using several thousand cartloads of stones taken from a stupendous 200ft (60m) diameter cairn that once stood on the shore, 'investing the little hamlet with the mysterious memorials and ghostly traditions of pre-historic times.' (McArthur, *The Antiquities of Arran*). As by far the largest monument in the area, it must have acted as a ritual focus. Many stone-lined cists were apparently disturbed and the bones discarded. One remaining cist, uncovered in 1900, yielded an early Bronze Age dagger and gold pommel-mount, now in the National Museum of Scotland. The cairn was on or near the present site of the building called Cairnhouse (NR89792814).

The Book of Arran 2 describes two death lights. About 1879 a strange light was seen almost nightly to rise at the mouth of the Blackwater and float along the shore. It was seen by many, and presumed to prefigure a drowning. Shortly afterwards a shoemaker named Callum went missing. Later another man (anonymised as S——) went missing and several people saw a light rise from the mouth of the Blackwater, float 200-300yds (183-274m) over to Cleit an Ruithe, then fly back to disappear or sink. It was about the size of a horse and was not seen anywhere else other than that part of the shore from Drumadoon Point to Blackwaterfoot. The light was never seen again after S—— was found on the shore, having drowned in the Blackwater.

Perhaps Blackwaterfoot's least likely claim to weirdness-related fame is its role in a spoof review of a non-existent fantasy series in a genuine fiction. To explain: in the tongue-in-cheek novel *The Warslayer; An Incredibly True Adventure Of Vixen The Slayer, The Beginning*, Rosemary Edghill created a character called Gloria McArdle, a former gymnast who plays a statuesque love goddess/ninja warrior in a television fantasy series called *Vixen the Slayer*, which is set in Elizabethan England but filmed in Australia. In the novel, Gloria is magically transported to a parallel world where the inhabitants believe she is a real monster-slayer, and, despite having no martial skills, she finds herself having to take on various supernatural threats. The whole thing is replete with knowing pop-culture references (*Galaxy Quest*, *Xena: Warrior Princess*, *Buffy the Vampire Slayer*), and as part of the book's fictional universe-within-a-universe it includes a joke episode guide to the Vixen TV series, written by Greg Cox (for whose Arran/*Star Trek* connection, see the chapter ARRAN AND POPULAR CULTURE). In episode eighteen, 'Sigh Of The Selkie,' Vixen comes to the aid of a seal-woman who has been captured by an unpleasant fisherman (the germ of the story may have come from the selkie tale just to the south – see CORRIECRAVIE). The unfortunate selkie is imprisoned in a caged metal tank and – in a parody of dolphin shows – is forced to perform tricks for her food. At one point a panel of stony-faced judges hold up signs scoring her performance. The spoof episode guide signs off with: 'Geographical Trivia Alert. The seaside village of Blackwaterfoot, where this episode is set, is a real place... you don't think the Slayer Staff could make up a name like that, do you?'

DRUMADOON/THE DOON★★

Blackwaterfoot is the starting point for a most enjoyable walk combining scenery, archaeology and a hint of weirdness. Start at the western end of the village by the golf course. Moving along the north-east edge of the course and crossing a fence into a field brings you to a ruined cairn at NR89112875. The capstone is huge and there are several stones in the area. The impressive nature of the site seeped into Fingalian folklore. Nigel Tranter, in *The Queen's Scotland: Argyll and Bute* claims it was thought to be the grave of Fingal's daughter, while John McArthur in *The Antiquities of Arran* says it was Ossian's daughter, Fingal's granddaughter, who was buried here. And the *Celtic Twilight* writer 'Fiona Macleod' (William Sharp) wrote of Ossian, 'nor does any know of his death, though the Gaels of the North believe that he looked his last across the grey seas from Drumadoon in Arran, where that Avalon of the Gael lies between the waters of Argyll and the green Atlantic wave' ('The Sunset of Old Tales', in *The Winged Destiny & Studies In The Spiritual History Of The Gael*).

Return to the clubhouse and strike west. If the tide is out you can walk along the beach. After about 700yds (640m) head north over a stile. To your left (the west) is the slope of the Iron Age hill fort called The Doon or Drumadoon. A gap in the defensive wall allows access to the inner area, and a single standing stone at NR88652927, claimed, as with the cairn further east, to mark the grave of Fingal's daughter. The interior has no other features, but is impressive for both its commanding position on Drumadoon Point, and its sheer size. It may have been a local tribal centre or oppidum. Martin Martin (*A Description of the Western Islands of Scotland circa 1695*) says, 'of old it was a sanctuary... whatever number of men or cattle could get within it, were secured from the assaults of enemies – the place being privileged by universal consent.' Return to the path via the same gap in the wall and continue north. The path

Left: Some of the columns of the 'shrinefield' north of Blackwaterfoot.

Below: The 'shrinefield', looking south to the cliffs of Drumadoon hillfort.

meets the beach, from where you can see the huge cliffs that form the fort's seaward defences. Further along the beach is one of the stranger sights on Arran. In what I have dubbed a shrinefield**, over 100 small columns of beach pebbles fill an area of around 150 square yards (137m²). Each column is typically four to seven pebbles high. There is no indication of the purpose of the constructions. Is it a place of religious dedications or thanksgiving? A prank? The output of a bored afternoon? Did someone put up the first one for ritual purposes or just for a laugh, and were others built simply through imitation, so that after a while a 'tradition' developed? I have no idea. It is a curious and fascinating place.

THE KING'S CAVE***

This superb and intriguing cave (NR88443092) can be reached by three paths – one coming north along the beach from The Doon, one leaving the car park on the main road at NR898315 and skirting the northern and then the western edges of the forestry plantation, and the new path directly west from the car park through the woods. A pair of legendary stories are attached to the cave. The first is that it was once home to Fingal, here represented not just as a hero but as a giant. Having built a bridge or set of stepping-stones between Arran and Kintyre, Fingal spent some R&R in the cave. His son was born here and McArthur (*The Antiquities of Arran*) says that a 2ft (61cm) long straight groove in the sandstone is the exact size of the child's foot the day after his birth. This would make the newborn 12ft (3.7m) high and his father 70-80ft (21-24m) tall. The other Fhiann lived in the associated caves alongside their chief, hunting across the island. Pennant (1772) records the belief that the obvious beam sockets at ceiling height near the entrance held wooden supports for the Fhiann's skin cooking bags, while Martin (1695) says they were used for 'holding big trees on which the caldrons hang.'

The most persistent current legend, however, is that Robert the Bruce took refuge in the cave on his way from Rathlin Island to the Scottish mainland, and it was here that he encountered the resilient spider whose persistence inspired him to never give up his quest for the crown – a quest which eventually led to the famous victory over the English at Bannockburn. The first reference to the King's Cave name – although there is no explanation or reference to Robert the Bruce – is in Robertson's *Tour* of 1768 (which only came to print in the *Proceedings of the Society of Antiquaries of Scotland* in 1898). Pennant, visiting in 1772, mentions Fingal but not Bruce. *The Statistical Account* of 1795 is the first widely-available work to record the tradition and this forms the key source for the enthusiasm of later writers, none of whom could resist the celebrity allure of the Bruce name. Soon the legend spread to placenames of the surrounding landscape, so that the smaller adjacent caves are supposedly the King's kitchen, cellars, larder and stable, and the high ground to the east being known as Torr Righ Mòr and Tigh Righ Beag, the 'big and little hillock of the King' respectively. But there is as much archaeological or documentary evidence for the association with Robert the Bruce as there is for the mythical Fingal.

It is, however, easy to see why the cave inspires legends: its walls are a treasure trove of old rock carvings. Unfortunately many of these are now obscured and confused by two centuries of graffiti and modern figures. Excavation has revealed nothing, and dating the carvings is little more than guesswork. Entry is through the metal gating,

Clockwise from top left: King's Cave entrance; one of the hunting dogs on the south wall of the south passage; deer, south wall of the south passage; the 'orans' praying figure, central buttress.

which was once kept locked but is now always open. Inside you find yourself in a large, irregular space about 120ft long and 30ft wide (36m x 9m), with a mostly flat dirt floor. A fair proportion of the interior is lit via the entrance, although you need to allow time for your eyes to adjust. To see the carvings a good torch is an advantage. The cave is shaped something like a bulbous Y, with two passages leading off at the far end, separated by a central buttress. This tour starts on the left (north) wall by the entrance and proceeds in a clockwise manner. It has to be said that without the detailed descriptions on the 'Canmore' website of the Royal Commission of Ancient and Historic Monuments of Scotland, I would not have been able to locate half of these carvings. Ian Fisher's *Early Medieval Sculpture in the West Highlands and Islands* has also proved invaluable.

North Wall

About 4½yds (4.1m) from the entrance are five serpents whose bodies form knots. These carvings – of which only the central three are obvious - are probably early medieval or Norse. Immediately left is an Ogham inscription about 20ins (50cm) long. Look for a vertical line with delicate horizontal and transverse marks. It may read EOMEQE, containing the Irish word 'meq' for 'son', but appears to be incomplete at both ends. A smaller possible inscription is just to the left; it is has proved resistant to transcription. A third Ogham is on the underside of the overhang 5ft (1.5m) to the right. It is about 1ft (30cm) long and may read LUEDBH, for which no interpretation can be given. These inscriptions are presumably early Christian, while a post-medieval date can be ascribed to the two masons' marks a further 11yds (10m) along. They have inverted arrows and one features a saltire. There are no carvings in the north passage.

Central Buttress

The most striking carving here is the large cross facing the entrance. It was interpreted by early visitors as a two-handed sword, and hence associated with Bruce. Impressive though it is, in terms of strangeness the cross cedes pride of place to the human figure to its right. The figure's arms are raised as if in the early Christian praying position called the 'orans', and hold a roughly semicircular arc – or two joined curves – above the head. Quite what is being held has given rise to a great deal of speculation. Suggestions have included a bow, two locks of hair and a rainbow. In the *Earth Mysteries* magazine 'Northern Earth' (No. 75), Grahame Sherbourne suggests a link with similar carvings of human figures holding or semi-haloed by bows or curves, found in Almeria (Spain), Askwith Moor in Yorkshire, and even in Hawaii. The figures are usually interpreted as hunters, wizards, priests or deities, although just as with the King's Cave carving, it's anyone's guess. Below the figure is an obvious mason's mark with an arrow rising from an 'M', and to the left of the cross is the largely lost carving of an animal. A small fish further to the left is modern.

South Passage

The north wall here has another mason's mark about 7yds or metres from the passage entrance. On the south wall opposite is a horse and rider, and above them a stylised galloping horse. Locate the house or tent carved at the mouth of the passage. Looking to the right you can see two hounds, possibly chasing the deer at the same level and further to the right. Moving right again is a hard-to-see orans figure similar to that on the central buttress. Lower down to the right are two concentric circles which are very suggestive of prehistoric cup and ring marks.

South Wall
The overhang by the cave mouth has two triangular-shaped 'shields', with another eroded shield or disc around 2yds (1.8m) to the right.

The Book of Arran 2 records the tradition of a secret passage from the King's Cave to another part of Arran. As is traditional in these 'Piper in the Tunnel' tales, a piper ventured in with his dog. After some distance he met Something Bad, because he was heard to pipe in Gaelic, 'Woe's me, woe is me, not having three hands, two for the pipe and one for the sword'. How you pipe such a lament while fending off Something Bad That Is Attacking You is beyond my comprehension. The piper was never seen again but the dog finally did return, only *sans* hair. For yet another hairless hound escaping subterranean jeopardy, see DIPPIN HEAD.

The natural tunnel or arch to the south – the 'King's Stable' – gives access to two smaller caves, the 'King's Kitchen' and 'Larder'. Both have artificial curves of boulders but their purpose or age has not been identified. A Norse interlace carving was discovered in the southernmost cave in 1993 when an unusually high tide removed some soil. It is on the north-east wall where the wall meets the floor. I have to say I was unable to find it.

TORMORE

This paragraph covers the prehistoric monuments between the King's Cave car park and Tormore, in the area south of the major ritual complex on Machrie Moor. The chambered cairn on the moorland east of the road (NR90313106), known as Tormore 1, is a Clyde group long cairn. The cairn material has gone, but the chamber is well-defined and the views to the mountains are superb. Two stones from an almost totally destroyed cist are built into the farm buildings of Rowanbank, (NR89453242) on the west side of the road.

MACHRIE MOOR★★★

We have never witnessed a wilder and more grandly solemn scene than these old circles on the Mauchrie Moor, looming in the shadowy indistinctness of an autumn moonlight... as we wandered amongst the old ruins, the weirdly stirring legends of the past haunted our mind, till the wreaths of mist seemed to float about like shadowy phantoms, and the circling monoliths and hoary cromlech appeared to rise from the heath, like ghosts of the heroes of old, bending around the grave of their buried chief. (John McArthur, *The Antiquities of Arran*)

The best group of architecturally varied stone circles in western Europe. (Aubrey Burl, *A Guide to The Stone Circles of Britain, Ireland and Brittany*)

Along with Stonehenge, Avebury, and the complexes on Lewis and Orkney, Machrie Moor is one of the best stone circle sites in the UK. In a highly concentrated area you can find seven stone circles, plus several chambered cairns, standing stones and hut circles. Allow plenty of time – the more you look, the more monuments you will find. The main grouping is about 1½ miles (2.4km) along a rough track east from the parking area ¼mile (400m) south of Machrie Bridge.

The complex represents ritual use of the landscape over thousands of years. The first monuments were timber circles, erected around 2500BC, at the start of the late Neolithic period. The largest of these timber circles had around fifty large posts arranged around an inner horseshoe of even taller timbers – it must have been a very impressive structure. The several timber circles continued in use for perhaps 500 years, and their erection clearly represented a new approach to religious ritual. To quote the interpretation panel on the site, they 'may have become arenas for more direct contact with the gods, circumventing the earlier role of ancestors.' Nothing can be seen of them now as around 2000BC, at the start of the Bronze Age, the timber structures were replaced with ritual monuments in stone – but not before the ground was ploughed in between. In some case standing stones were placed in the exact locations of the timber postholes, even though these postholes should have been obliterated by the ploughing. This suggests the ploughing was not agricultural but ritual in purpose – perhaps a 'cleansing' or 'rededication' of the sacred ground before the stone circles were erected, creating an 'outdoor temple' ceremonial complex with multiple sites within just a few paces of each other. Great effort was spent on locating the stone circles in precise positions, as archaeologists have found that their sites exploit the natural variations in the landscape to ensure they can be seen from as far and wide as possible – if you stand at Circle 6, for example, you can see Circles 1, 2, 3 and 5.

Over just one day – 24 May 1861 – James Bryce heroically dug into five of the circles, and the site continues to be a focus of major archaeological investigations to this day. Most of the circles have been found to contain a small number of burials, presumably of important people. This seems to represent a change in burial practice – the earlier Neolithic chambered cairns were collective burial monuments for the community, whereas the new rites valorised the individual. During a period lasting perhaps 1,800-2,000 years the circles, timber or stone, were in a sacred precinct, set apart from the concerns of ordinary life – settlements have been found to the west and south of the complex, but the area of the circles themselves clearly remained inviolate. Eventually however, the site was abandoned, probably due to the deterioration in the climate, which caused the area to be blanketed with bogs. So extensive was the peat that one circle – Number 11 – was only re-discovered through subsurface probing in the 1970s.

Such an impressive grouping of mysterious stones could not fail to attract folklore. McArthur in *The Antiquities of Arran* gives two origin myths. In one a quorum of fairies convened on the summit of Durra-na-each (modern day Dereneneach, over-looking the moor on the high ground east of the String road at NR931331). To pass the time they devised a game of flicking pebbles using only the finger and thumb onto the plain below. The 'pebbles' are of course the grey granite boulders and red sandstone pillars of the stone circles. The alternative version has Fingal and the Fheinn hunting boar in the woods of Arran when they are interrupted by a Viking raiding party. In the ensuing battle the Celtic heroes triumphed, but not without some losses, and their dead were buried on Machrie Moor, with the circles of stone raised over the graves to mark them for evermore.

The stark monuments were also a suitable setting for supernatural encounters. *The Book of Arran 2* tells of Domhnull (Donald) nam mogan, a religious man from Tormore, who was traveling home late one night when he met a bocan near the stones. The entity was so huge Donald could see all of the mountain of Ard Bheinn between its legs. Donald asked that it assume the size and appearance it had when living on earth, and when this happened Donald recognized it as the spirit of a man he once knew (although the account doesn't say who this was). Donald then interrogated the bocan: did it know what had happened to Angus Dubh when he was lost on a journey between Lamlash and Shisken via Clachan Glen? The bocan denied having anything to do with the episode, but did reveal who had hurled Angus over a certain cliff. Donald then asked to be shown a treasure, and was told to come to a spot in GLEANN-AN-T-SUIDHE the next night, but without his darning needle in his bonnet, his little dog and the ball of worsted in his pocket. The following day Donald cautiously took advice, and did not keep the appointment. See also THE STRING ROAD for more about Donald and the bocan. In *The Isle of Arran Mystery*, Lady Penelope and Parker discover a clue carved on the 'third stone to the right' of one of the circles, although we are not told which circle (see the ARRAN AND POPULAR CULTURE chapter).

There are so many circles and other monuments in the area that it is easy to become disoriented. This tour starts from the road and proceeds east along the track. The numbers given to the circles follow the current convention, such as is used in the on-site Historic Scotland interpretation (some earlier works use a different system, and this is also referred to where appropriate). Note that the moor is very exposed in bad weather and the track is often muddy. Access by wheelchair is just about possible if you have a good reserve of dedication.

Machrie Moor – The Tour

When you pass through the first fence along the track, the area to the right is the Mesolithic site of Balnagore. There used to be a lambing pen here, which caused the ground to be worked over every spring, so uncovering many flint and pitchstone tools from the hunter-gatherer encampment. There is nothing to see now. About ½mile (800m) along the track you come to the first monument, Moss Farm Road Stone Circle★★ (NR90063265). In some earlier works this is also called Circle 10. The course of the track originally cut through the north side of the mound and the site has been quarried for building materials for the nearby dykes. Nevertheless, it is a still impressive monument, with twelve stones forming a perimeter around a large central cairn mound about 22yds (20m) across. As the interpretation panel notes, there is some dispute about what the site actually is – is it a stone circle surrounding a burial cairn that was inserted later, or is it just a cairn with a large kerb of stones? In *The Antiquities of Arran* McArthur describes a 'partly demolished cairn' which he identifies as Fingal's court of justice. This is probably it.

Carry along the track – passing a bush with a fine growth of the yellow fungus called Witch's Butter – until the third fence comes in to view. A small but visible path runs north (left) to a solitary standing stone★, 5ft 4ins (1.6m) tall with a weathered top (NR90643253). In 1861 McArthur mentioned several smaller stones nearby, apparently fragments of larger ones, possibly indicating the existence of a former stone circle. Bryce dug a trench to try and locate this circle, but found nothing. It is likely that McArthur was confusing this site with the single remaining stone and broken

Moss Farm Road stone circle.

Standing stone north of the track. The Boscawen memorial is within the fenced enclosure in the background.

stumps of Circle 3. In connection with Fingal's 'court of justice', *The New Statistical Account* of 1845 notes that: 'The stone on which the culprit stood is still pointed out, and called the Panel's stone.' The 'Panel' is the word used in the Scottish justice system for the accused. Given that the 'court' is likely to be the Moss Farm Road Circle to the west, and the other circles are some considerable distance away, I believe this is probably the 'Panel's stone' (where the Panel probably pleaded Standard Excuse #1, 'It wasnae me. A big boy did it and ran away, mister.'). On the other hand, you can't stand on this stone, so perhaps both Fingal's court of justice, and the Panel's stone, are the tumbled boulders of Tormore 2? (See below.)

Just behind the solitary stone, within a wooden enclosure, is a modern monument to John Boscawen (1906-1972), with the inscription: 'He gloried in the high tops/Found his peace in the hush of the glen/Brodick garden was his inspiration/And all nature his friend.' Around it is a hut-circle (NR90663254). Between the standing stone and the main track is another, reasonably obvious, hut-circle. Continue along the track to two large stones at right angles to each other. This is all that remains of the burial chamber of Moss Farm Cist (NR90573237). In the field to the right (the south), you can see another upright stone. This is Tormore 2 chambered cairn (NR90633224), reachable via a stile and a short walk. It is very badly damaged, with just two stones still standing and a barely recognisable chamber. In summer it is swamped in bracken. Everything up to now, however, has just been the warm-up act. Return to the track and continue to the disused buildings of Moss Farm, where the main event begins.

Circle 5*** (NR90883235)

This striking monument of two concentric circles stands just to the right of the path. The inner ring is 40ft (12m) in diameter and has eight stones, while the outer possesses fifteen. All the stones are grey granite boulders, probably glacial deposits found on site. McArthur excavated in 1858, removing 4ft (1.2m) of stones without reaching the ground surface. Three years later Bryce removed another foot (30cm) of material and found two flat stones on edge, apparently the remains of a ruined central cist.

Moss Farm Cist. (courtesy of Ségolène Dupuy)

Tormore 2 chambered cairn, south of the track.

Circle 5, the double concentric ring. The holed stone is in the right foreground.

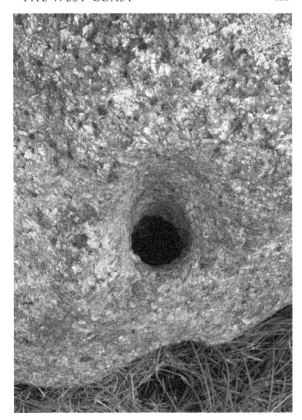

Circle 5, the hole where Fingal's dogs Bran and Scaolain were tied (or the fairy's milk funnel). (courtesy of Ségolène Dupuy)

Folklorically, the circle is known as Suide Choir Fhionn, Fingal's Cauldron Seat, where the giant/hero cooked up a tasty repast. The low boulder on the southern edge of the outer circle, opposite the vaguely phallic stone of the inner circle, has a round through-hole in its edge. Two reasons are given for its existence: its sides were worn smooth by the leads used to tether Fingal's dogs Bran and Scaolain, or, as noted by McArthur (*The Antiquities of Arran*), the circle was home to a fairy or brownie who could only be propitiated by pouring milk through the hole. The Dragon Project, a programme to measure 'earth energies' at megalithic sites, found that Circle 5 gave a significantly higher radiation count than the other monuments, but no real significance could be found in the results.

Circle 4★ (NR91003235)

This small circle, a 'four-poster', stands about 110yds (100m) east-north-east of Circle 5. The four stones are distinctively the same type of white granite boulders, and are likely to be glacial erratics found on the moor. In 1861 Bryce found a small central cist containing the remains of a crouched inhumation burial, some 3ft (91cm) below the ground surface. A food vessel, bronze pin, three flakes of flint and fragments of bone were recovered. The description in *The New Statistical Account* of a monument 'in the shape of a parallelogram' probably applies to this site, which makes it the supposed grave of Fingal's dog (but was it Bran or Scaolain?).

Circle 4, the Four Poster. Circle 2 can be seen in the distance. (courtesy of Ségolène Dupuy)

Circle 3★★★ (NR91013245)

This circle is around 110yds (100m) north of Circle 4. One spectacularly large slab of vertically grooved red sandstone still stands, the stumps and broken fragments of three others are still visible, and five fallen stones lurk beneath the surface. One of the stumps has an intriguing central cavity – this may simply be the remains of a leverage hole made by whoever toppled the stone, or, possibly, it suggests this stone had a notch or through-hole.

In contrast to the low granite boulders of Circles 5 and 4, which were probably found in the immediate area and not worked by tools, the tall thin sandstone slabs of Circle 3 were quarried some distance away (possibly at Auchencar, 3 miles (5km) to the north-west) and deliberately shaped. Bryce found two cists, one containing the skeleton of a twenty-two-year-old man, two flints and a pot which disintegrated on recovery, while the second contained two flints and the residue of a crouched burial. From the size of the stumps and fragments it is clear the lost stones were probably a similar size to the remaining upright. There may not be much left of this circle, but what remains is quite wonderful. In its pomp it must have been one of the most impressive circles in the country.

Circle 2★★★ (NR91133242)

Circle 2 is to the east of Circle 3 and is impossible to miss, the triumvirate of red sandstone pillars being visible for a great distance, and the tallest stone being 18ft (5.5m) high. This is the iconic Arran stone circle. There were probably originally another four or five megaliths – one has been cut in two and the halves partially converted into millstones which are still *in situ*, and which were described by Headrick in 1807. It is intriguing to speculate what caused the abandonment of this labour. Was there

Circle 3, the sole remaining upright stone, with Circle 2 in the background.

Circle 3, the 'holed' stump of one of the fallen stones. (courtesy of Ségolène Dupuy)

Circle 2, the upper image also shows the abandoned millstones made from toppled stones of the circle.

a suggestion that grinding stones created from such a source would have an ill effect on the grain? Or was it simply that, on a practical level, the stones didn't shape up as planned? Like Circle 3, the sandstone slabs were quarried and brought a distance to be erected here. If they were deliberately shaped, one wonders what the notch at the bottom of the central stone was for. Excavation in 1861 by Bryce found two cists, one central, the other between the centre and the current north-eastern pillar. Neither of them had any bones remaining.

Circle 1** (NR91203239)

This lies about 55yds (50m) east-south-east of Circle 2. This is one of the circles that has been subject to thorough modern archaeological excavation and so we know more about it than many of the others. The first ritual use of the site predates the circle-building era – a number of pits were dug around 4300-3500BC. When excavated these were found to contain broken Neolithic pottery, charcoal, flakes of flint and pitchstone, and hazelnut shells. The exact purpose of these deposits remains a mystery, although they are possibly related to burials or the dead in some way. Then came a complex of timber circles. The outermost was a ring of thirty-four posts, 66ft (20m) in diameter (by contrast, the current circle is 46ft (14m) across). This enclosed a smaller ring of sixty-three posts with a diameter of around 49ft (15m), within which was a setting of five posts. Around 2000BC stones replaced timbers. Within the circle was a pit with an inverted cinerary urn which contained the cremated remains of an adult (probably male) who was somewhat less than thirty years old at death, plus a flint knife and a bone pin.

Until quite recently the eleven stones (from an original twelve) were always considered to alternate between elongated sandstone slabs and granite boulders. However an article in *Current Archaeology* (No.176, October/November 2001), written by geologist Ian Meighan and archaeologist Derek Simpson, established that the sandstone had been misidentified, and the vertical blocks were in fact another form of granite

Circle 1, showing the variation between elongated and rounded stones.

– a finer-grained granite than the coarse granite that made up the boulders. This lithological identification enabled the different stones to be traced to their sources. The round-edges of the coarse granite boulders showed they were ice-transported glacial erratics found on site at Machrie, but the angular finer-grain granite blocks had been moved by humans from an area a few miles/kilometres away. So the builders of Circle 1 clearly believed it was for some reason important to drag the fine-grained slabs that distance. Meighan and Simpson conclude that the reason was sexual symbolism based on shape, the small elongated (male) stones contrasting with the larger rounded (female) stones. A similar sexual dimorphism between alternating stones is found in the famous West Kennet Avenue at Avebury, and also in stone rows and avenues elsewhere in Britain and Ireland. The symbolism suggests Circle 1 was associated with a fertility cult.

Circle 6** (NR91213241)

Circle 6 is just to the north-east of Circle 1. In some accounts it is also known as Circle 11 or Circle 1a. This circle was partially recorded in the nineteenth century, but then disappeared under peat, to be rediscovered through probing in 1975 and only finally revealed by excavation in 1985 and 1986. 42ft (13m) across, it has ten small upright stones (nine of sandstone and one of granite) and six buried stones. Like Circle 1, the earliest ritual phase involved Neolithic pits containing broken pottery, followed by a timber circle with ten uprights, just a little larger than the current circle. The shape of the stone circle is unconventional – not a circle or an oval at all – and may even be two semi-circles of stones joined together. A cremation burial was found in a central pit, containing the remains of an individual who was probably male and aged about thirty. During very wet conditions part of the circle may be under water.

Circle 6, partly under water after rain. In the distance can be seen, from left to right, Circles 5, 2 and 3. (courtesy of Ségolène Dupuy)

A small path leaves Circle 6 to the east, allowing access to the two damaged four-poster stone circles near the String Road (see BALLYMICHAEL).

A small (2ft high) isolated standing stone stands to the south of the main complex at NR91043224. It does not appear to have been part of a circle and, as the RCAHMS 'Canmore' website gently puts it, 'its purpose and origin are uncertain,' suggesting the possibility that it may not be prehistoric. In 'The Great Stone Circles Project,' an article in *British Archaeology* (No. 81, March/April 2005) Colin Richards describes the rediscovery of another probable stone circle to the north of Circles 2 and 3. In 1832 James Skene had sketched a single standing monolith in this area. It was subsequently destroyed, but Richards' team found the broken stump, 'a substantial piece of red sandstone.' If it does represent a complete circle, and said circle was consistent with the others, then it would have been another ring of tall red monoliths. As archaeological work continues, it is possible other sites will emerge from the moor.

From time to time suggestions have been made that the circles have alignments on astronomical events. In 1978 John Barnett suggested that Circles 1, 2 4 and 11 were in general alignment on the very prominent notch to the north-east, where Machrie Glen divides into two – the notch being where, at the time of the construction of the circles, the midsummer sun rose. Within five minutes of the sun leaving the horizon, it would be also be visible from Circles 3 and 5. Every nineteen years there is a lunar cycle during which the full moon appears to 'stand still' in the sky, and some stone circles – notably Callanish on Lewis – definitely seem to be constructed to align on this event. Barnett claimed that the Machrie Glen notch also indicated the rising winter full moon at the minor standstill (as seen from Circles 3 and 5), and a second notch to the north-west, visible only from Circle 5, marks the setting winter full moon at the time of the major standstill. It has to be said that not everyone accepts these astro-archaeological conclusions, but they remain possibilities and speculations replete with interest.

MACHRIE

This paragraph deals with the area north of the Machrie Water and Machrie Bridge, which although being known as 'Machrie' is quite distinct from Machrie Moor. A single standing stone can be seen looking east from the road north of the bridge over the Machrie Water (NR89453363). A forestry track leading north just east of Machrie Farm (on the road joining the coast road with The String) takes you to several more seldom-visited monuments and prehistoric sites surrounded by forestry. Follow the track uphill. About 650yds (600m) after the second gate you come to clearing on your right. Keep to the left, and follow the southern edge of the trees to reach a second clearing after about 100yds (90m) ring. Turn left here to see two hut circles. Cross the clearing diagonally to the right for a third clearing with a standing stone (NR91013455). The depressions in the stone look like manmade cupmarks but are in fact natural. Return to the main track and continue uphill until it levels out and starts to go downhill. Just to right of track is a small four-poster stone circle (NR90813508). Return by the way you came.

AUCHENGALLON★★

A signposted track leads to this Historic Scotland-owned site, which is both wonderful and enigmatic in equal measure. It consists of a central grassy mound surrounded by a circle of fifteen upright stones of different shapes, sizes and rock type. The hillside location (NR89283464) gives superb views over Kilbrannan Sound, some of the stones are weathered into fantastic shapes, and the whole site has a wonderful atmosphere. The enigma comes with what Auchengallon actually is. The standard view is that it is a Bronze Age burial cairn with the 'stone circle' forming a kerb. The RCAHMS 'Canmore' website then lists its possible alternative history. In 1864 the Ordnance Survey surveyor stated that the interior of the stone circle was filled with loose stones gathered from the adjacent fields, and in *The Book of Arran 1* (1910) Mr Archibald Sim, a long-time local inhabitant, told the archaeologists that in his youth – which may have been the 1860s – 'the enclosed area was flat and free of stones… the stones gathered from the fields have been piled year after year within it, until now a number of the upright stones are actually hidden below them.' In other words, the monument is not a cairn but a stone circle whose centre had been filled with modern field clearance stones. 'Canmore' rounds off the episode by noting that: 'It is doubtful that the compacted mass of turf-covered stones that form the cairn could be of entirely recent origin.' So it's probably a burial cairn and kerb. If the light is right, you might find that the largest stone on the northern edge bears the simulacrum of a ghostly face.

AUCHENCAR/DRUID

The cliffs above the road north of Auchengallon bristle with caves. Between the road and the cliff (NR892357) is a very small burial ground★. This is a strange, almost desolate place, many of the nineteenth-century gravestones having worn away to mere stumps, and much of the site is under water in wet weather. The enclosing wall is clearly later than the graves, and was presumably built to protect them from

Opposite: Auchengallon kerb cairn, looking south.

This page: The stones of the kerb at Auchengallon, and Auchencar standing stone, the tallest on Arran.

animals. Sadly it has not prevented the activities of teenagers, who have left a 'party layer' as a record of their visits. To the north, the single-track road to Auchencar (look for the sign to the Old Byre) gives a terrific view of the thin pointy standing stone★★ near Druid, at 16ft 5ins (5m) high the tallest on Arran (NR 89053633). Its twin lies flat nearby, broken into three pieces. The two massive stones must together have been an incredible sight. Cross into the field by the stile. Aubrey Burl identified a site nearby as a possible quarry for some of the sandstone monoliths on Machrie Moor.

DOUGARIE/GLEN IORSA

In 1983 pupil Kirsty McEachern recorded rumours that a Grey Lady haunts Dougarie Lodge (NR 884371) at night and that a stagecoach passed the lodge at midnight (Arran Heritage Community Group, *Isle of Arran Heritage*). The lodge's owner, the Anglo-Irish Lord Rossmore, was said to have gambled away the shooting lodge when drunk, and the Duke of Hamilton refused to give it back. Ah, aristocrats. (This story may alternatively apply to the former lodge at CATACOL).

Two young women took the cows to the summer shieling on the upper part of Loch Iorsa (NR 913379). When they had enough butter and cheese ready one girl would return to the farm with the produce, leaving the other girl alone. One night a strange woman asked for shelter having lost her way. The lone girl was suspicious but let her in, even though the dog immediately went and hid. The tall stranger went to bed but the girl sat up, worried. To her horror she saw that a black hoof stretched out from under the woman's bedclothes. She quietly stole out and ran off with the dog. The hoofed woman followed. The dog attacked but it made no difference. The girl just managed to get to her father's house and bar the door in the big woman's face, but the dog was left outside and was found next morning hairless and in pieces. The tale is in *The Book of Arran 2*.

WHITEFARLAND

There is a small but very interesting graveyard between the beach and the road (NR 86374192), just south of Whitefarland. A little to the north of the cemetery (NR 86474219) a Late Bronze Age gold armlet was dug up in 1921, and very close by (NR 865424) is a coastal bank in which the sea exposed several burial cists during the first sixty years of the nineteenth century. The knoll of Cnoc a' Chaibeil (hill of the chapel, NR 86604230) behind the houses of Whitefarland is supposed to have been a burying place at some undetermined time in the past.

THUNDERGAY

Near the small complex of buildings at Mid Thundergay is Tobar Challumchille (St Columba's Well, NR 88074659). The spring has an enclosing brick wall. Other than the name, no folklore or other association with Columba, Scotland's greatest saint, has come down to us; it is one of the intriguingly few Columban names on Arran, all of which exist in isolation without any supporting tradition. Further north the tiny Lenimore Cemetery stands at the eastern side of the road (NR 88354756).

CATACOL

This tiny hamlet has a significant role in Arran's rich fantasy-world of placenames and speculative history. Down by the shore at NR91134948 there was once a circular prehistoric cairn. Its name, according to John McArthur's 1861 book *The Antiquities of Arran*, was Aran, which he reworks as 'Ar Fhinn', meaning 'the slaughter of Fingal'. McArthur's story – apparently based on an eighteenth-century poem – is that the cairn was raised to commemorate the death of Manos, King of Sweden (or the son of the King). Manos invaded Arran, but was disarmed and captured by Fingal, who released him on his honour that he would trouble the island no more. But almost immediately the Norseman returned with his galleys, and was killed in battle by Fingal. Nigel Tranter (*The Queen's Scotland: Argyll and Bute*) says the name of the Viking prince was Arin, from which the name Arran was derived. And *The Book of Arran 2* interprets the name Catacol as either Katta-gil, meaning wild cats' gully, or, Kati, small ship, 'in favour of the legend that Magnus Berfaettr and his men landed here to avenge an insult by Fingal'. Whatever the truth or otherwise of any of this, *The New Statistical Account* of 1845 noted a road had been cut through the cairn, and its stones re-used in the construction. Nothing now remains.

The key feature of Catacol is the row of whitewashed adjacent cottages known as the Twelve Apostles, or The Row. Today they have an idyllic air, but their history is dark. In 1840 Henry Westenra, Lord Rossmore, husband of Anne Douglas, the illegitimate daughter of the 7th Duke of Hamilton, built a shooting lodge in the area (it is now Catacol farmhouse). The only trouble was the unsightly locals and their unsightly houses spoiled the toffs' view. Rossmore built The Row (then called Arrandale) and tried to persuade them to move. To a person the villagers refused. What happened next varies on who is telling the story. In one version his lordship waited until all the younger men, who followed parallel occupations of farmer and fisher, were at sea. In another, he invited the local fishermen to a meeting or party at the lodge and then had his servants bar the door. Whatever the process, the result was the same – eighty-five people had their houses burned. The tenants, not surprisingly, refused to kowtow to such an action, and ignored The Row, preferring to scatter all over the island or move to Kintyre. A few tried to return to their former homes, but were evicted following legal action in the courts by Lady Rossmore, the actual owner of the land. Ah, aristocrats (again). The mordant foundations of Old Catacol can be clearly seen about mile (1km) east of the road, along the track leading past Catacol Farm.

Some years before 1861 an urn containing silver coins and a gold chain was dug up from beneath a large stone on Catacol Farm (NR911495). The finds were sold to a goldsmith in Ardrossan. In 1936 a stone-lined grave was found somewhere in the farm's fields. It was oriented east-west and so was presumably Christian. The skeleton was much decayed. An anonymous manuscript, quoted on the RCAHMS 'Canmore' website, says: 'The rough structure of the grave and its situation would seem to point to an isolated sepulture, the result perhaps of some sudden death or tragedy.' Also in 1936 an iron rod, 170cm (almost 7ins) long and about 2mm (0.08ins) in diameter was found in a stone grave (possibly the same one?) by John Robertson of Catacol Farm. The object has not been identified; it is in Brodick Castle.

To the south-east, above the glen of the Abhainn Mor, is a small boulder-strewn spur called Clach a' Chait, the Cat Stone (NR918490). This is supposed to be where the last victim of a running battle between Cromwellian troops and the people of

Arran was killed. The alternative, and more widely quoted, versions of the skirmish are that it took place around either BRODICK CASTLE or the other Cat Stone at CORRIE on the east coast.

North-east of Catacol, on the high ground of Cnoc an Uird at NR91785046, there is a hut circle, a cairn, the footings of shielings, a large fallen stone and a standing stone 2.5ft (0.75m) high, which may be a boundary marker.

'The Sailor's Grave. Here lies John Mclean Died 12 August 1854.' This is the inscription on a stone in front of a grassy cairn at the north end of the parking area (part of the former road) north-west of Catacol at NR918508. There is a small upright stone at the head of the grave. The story of John Mclean and his death has several variations. One – told by Mrs Nettie Anderson from Lochranza in the Arran Heritage Community Group's book *Isle of Arran Heritage* – says he died of cholera on board a ship. He was taken ashore and buried in a hurriedly dug isolated grave, this being in accordance with the law that said a person who died of the disease in the night had to be buried next morning. A second version, taken from the website of the Castlekirk B&B in Lochranza, dates the episode to 1854. John Mclean had died on board a ship anchored in the bay off Lochranza. The people of the village fearfully refused to allow the plague-corpse to be buried in their churchyard; it was the same story at Catacol. Eventually the body was interred half way between the two. It became a custom for people to leave a beach pebble on the sailor's grave as they passed by. An alternative, and much more suspiciously dramatic version, is that the ship's crew stranded Mclean here because he was ill with a deadly infectious disease. He tried to obtain help from both Lochranza and Catacol, but was turned away from both places. Starving and sick, he died by the road, and was buried on the spot by the local people. Perhaps inevitably, his ghost is said to walk between the two villages, constantly seeking assistance that will never come.

Catacol – the Sailor's Grave.

8

THE NORTH-EAST COAST, FROM LOCHRANZA TO CORRIE

LOCHRANZA

Lochranza folks have caught an occasional glimpse of a 'ghost' recently, says a correspondent. Lochranza may congratulate itself; the fact of this reported mysterious visitant having selected the locality as winter quarters is another evidence of the wide appreciation of the improved water supply. (*Ardrossan & Saltcoats Herald*, 12 February 1897)

This scenic village has a number of places of interest, as well as being the most common location on the island to see golden eagles and red deer (for the latter, try the golf course). The castle★ (NR933507, Historic Scotland, free entry, interpretation panels) stands proud on a spit of land jutting scenically out into the sea loch. It is one of the locations for the clues found in *The Isle of Arran Mystery* (see the ARRAN AND POPULAR CULTURE chapter). Lochranza church★ (NR93695021), in the centre of the village, was built in 1795 on the site of an earlier establishment. The field to the south is called Achadh an Teampuill, 'the field of the temple or church'. A gravestone with skull and cross bones, dated 1685, and originally in the floor of the church, is built into the east gable. The graveyard contains a small number of other carved stones.

The Arran Whisky Distillery Visitor Centre has an audio-visual film on the story of whisky on the island, and some artefacts of the illegal stills. Saint Bride's Chapel (also known as St James') once stood at the bottom end of the village, on the north side of the burn (NR94494993). This was a simple chapel and burial ground which disappeared in the 1830s. It achieved a spurious fame, however, when Sir Walter Scott, in his 1814 verse epic *The Lord of the Isles*, aggrandised it as the 'convent' where Robert the Bruce met his sister Lady Isabel, the 'Maid of Lorn'. A case can be made for saying that Scott invented much of what is now popularly regarded as 'truth' in Scottish history – not deliberately, because he was writing novels and romances, but because they were so popular that his vast readership started to see the Scottish landscape through the lens of Scott's works. This is one example. Scott had taken the events in Barbour's medieval saga *The Bruce* and created a fictional romance, but in the words of Robert McLellan in *The Isle of Arran*, 'later visitors thrilled to the idea that... they were on the site of the nunnery of St Bride, where the sister of Bruce had spent her days in prayer, having renounced forever the love of a man whom she considered betrothed to another.'

In his 1902 book *Evil Eye in the Western Highlands* R.C. MacLagan described the origin of the evil eye: 'The natural irritation felt at the hostile look of a neighbour,

Lochranza Castle, with stag.

Lochranza church – gravestone
from 1685 affixed to the gable.

still more of an enemy, is implanted in the breast of all, however much they may be influenced by moral teaching.' He went on to describe the story of a Lochranza man who had involuntary cronachadh (the evil eye). No matter what he looked at – a new-born animal, a field of crops – his look would blast or cronach it. A lad from another part of the island wanted to marry this man's daughter. When the lad's neighbours heard this they protested, as they didn't want his offspring in the area 'to cronach everything about the place'.

The Book of Arran 2 tells of a hunchbacked weaver from Lochranza who was cutting brackens on the hill one day when he came across a group of fairies dancing in a green secluded hollow. They were singing, 'Monday Tuesday; Monday Tuesday.' He jumped to his feet and shouted, 'and Wednesday'. The fairies liked this suggestion so much they added it to their song, and also removed his hump and placed it on the turf dyke. Hearing of this, another hunchbacked weaver went to see the fairies and called out, 'Thursday Friday Saturday'. The fairies were deeply annoyed and transferred the first man's hump on his chest. This tale is so widespread I doubt there is an area of the Highlands and Islands where it is not told. It is also found in Ireland, Cornwall and Brittany, and even in Japan where the transferred disability is a wen not a hump.

The following story is taken from the website of the Castlekirk B&B in Lochranza, www.castlekirk.co.uk; the original source was a local storyteller, and the incident, it is said, took place in Lochranza in the 1950s. A girl, walking around the head of the loch, encountered a blond young man sitting on an old fence. There was something strange about him, as if he was not from that time, so she decided to avoid him, but he shouted, and in an instant she somehow found herself standing next to him. He produced a beautiful, ornately-decorated comb and asked if she had lost such a thing. 'Not me,' she replied. Twice more he asked her the same question, each time his voice climbing in hypnotic intensity. Resisting the narcotic, enchanting power of his voice, she replied in the negative each time, although the last refusal required a real effort of will. Then he gave her the comb, but she quickly handed it back. At this, the intensity seemed to drain out of the encounter and, now looking sad and wistful, the young man asked, 'Then will you do just one thing for me… comb my hair?' The girl acquiesced to this but as she combed his golden locks, sand, seashells and starfish fell from his head. Now filled with fear, the lass dropped the comb and ran for her life, breathlessly telling the story to her parents when she reached home. Her mother and father went at once to investigate, but back at the scene there was no sign of the man, just a small collection of shells and starfish, and a handful of very white sand forming a triskelion or triskele. (The triskelion is an ancient three-legged symbol which Robert Graves, in The White Goddess, his study of mythology, identifies as a lunar symbol, a representation of the three phases of the Triple Goddess – Maiden, Mother, Crone; how it fits in with this story is not clear, other than that the Moon is intimately connected to the sea.) An old woman from Lochranza told the girl that she had had a very lucky escape, for the stranger was clearly the Sea God of the Celts, Manannan Mac Lir, and every seven years he came ashore to take a human woman to his underwater fastness.

The motif of finding seaweed, sand or starfish in the hair of a handsome stranger is widespread in Scotland – on the Western Isles he is usually Manannan, while on the inland lochs he typically turns out to be a water horse in his duplicitous human guise. In neither case are the shapeshifting individuals to be trusted, as their purpose is to abduct the human concerned, either for mating or food.

The Arran Heritage Community Group book contains a story told in 1991 by Bobby Taylor to his granddaughter Linda Taylor. There was an accident at sea on the Lochranza sailing smack *The Fairy Dell* and Nigel Kerr's brother was drowned. It was often said that his guiding spirit appeared when the boat was in danger. One night she was moored without any lights outside Rothesay Pier. A paddle steamer called *The Mercury* came within collision distance, but at the last minute there had been a strange glimmer of light. Bobby Taylor was at the wheel of *The Mercury*, saw the light, and avoided the smaller craft. *The Fairy Dell* was launched in 1897 and in 1931, when she was one of the last two sailing smacks remaining, and had her life prolonged through the fitting of a small engine. Allan Paterson Milne, in *Arran: An Island's Story,* quotes Robert Simper's *Scottish Sail: A Forgotten Era* on the boat's supernatural guardian: 'During a storm Captain Angus Kerr, her skipper-owner, was knocked or thrown overboard while conning *The Fairy Dell* through the gale. Coming up on deck the mate found a deserted helm and no trace of the captain. From then on a ghostly presence haunted *The Fairy Dell*. Those who sailed on her began to sense that they did not sail alone. Whenever the smack ran into trouble, the spirit of Captain Kerr came to the rescue, steering her with a firm but invisible hand.'

Milne's researches, however, produced a rather different take on the episode. Angus Kerr was indeed the captain, but he did not drown. Instead he retired from the sea and lived to a ripe old age in Lochranza where he was a pillar of the kirk. He sold the smack to Nigel Kerr, and it was Nigel's crewmate Findlay Kerr who went overboard somewhere off the Gourock-Wemyss Bay coast. As Milne says: 'The Lochranza Kerrs are a proliferating tribe, prone to confuse the researcher.' Nigel Kerr seemed dogged by bad luck. He rammed into the porthole of a small steamer in Rothesay Bay and could not get free until the steamer had been lowered to one side – which seems to be a different version of Bobby Taylor's story above. He could not find a regular crewmate to replace Findlay and eventually his wife had to crew alongside him, which gave rise to the usual muttering about women bringing bad luck to a fishing vessel. It is not clear where the ghost of Findlay Kerr fits into this, but Nigel Kerr's string of unfortunate incidents may have engendered the idea of a 'curse' on *The Fairy Dell*, which may in turn have given birth to the notion of a 'guardian spirit' which countered the curse.

The road south-east out of Lochranza through Glen Chalmadale passes over the Witches Bridge (NR959492). This is one of those places with a supernatural name that has no associated story that I can trace. Further up the road the layby at the top of the hill (NR973484) is the best place to see the 'sleeping warrior', a simulacrum formed by the shape of the hills to the west. His helmet is on the right, then comes nose and chin, the arms folded over his chest, and finally the legs. He is best seen silhouetted against a sunset or a clear blue sky

THE COCK OF ARRAN COASTAL WALK

This section deals with the coastal walk from Lochranza to Sannox. The easy 7½ mile (12km) walk is well worth doing but, as with everywhere else on Arran, proper footwear and weatherproof clothing is a must.

From Lochranza, take the minor road opposite the Field Study Centre and follow it through South Newton on the east side of the sea loch. The path which runs below

Lochranza – folklore in signs.

Fake stone circle near the Fairy Dell, east of Lochranza.

Ossian's Cave
– carving of
a ship.

the cliffs passes a very well constructed modern fake stone circle★ of ten small irregular stones and an off-centre flat stone (NR934517). Further to the east is the area
called the Fairy Dell – perhaps the circle was constructed because someone thought
the inhabitants of the Dell needed a place of rendezvous? The Cock of Arran itself
(NR958522) is a large rock on the beach; it was once a simulacrum, resembling a cock
with wings extended as if to crow, and was a notable landmark for sailors. Sadly the
'head' is long gone and it is no longer much of a curiosity.

Another five minutes walking brings you to Ossian's Cave★, although it is very
easy to miss. Look for a diagonal shelving of rock about 55yds (50m) west of the path
and then move left until you see a small cleft. The vestibule has two eighteenth- or
nineteenth-century ships carved on the north wall, along with more recent graffiti.
A narrow passage then leads into the inner cave, with a jumble of rocks forming
the uneven floor of a reasonably large cavern. Don't venture in if you don't care for
completely lightless spaces. Or spiders. In terms of the name, I can find no link with
Ossian (Fingal's son) or the other Fingalians. Note that the cave is shown in the wrong
position (NR96285169) on the 1:25000 Ordnance Survey map, although it appears to
be in the right spot on the 1:50000. The correct grid reference is NR96025181.

Further south are the ruins of a small eighteenth-century industrial complex where
salt was produced by boiling seawater (NR971511). The low-grade coal was mined on
the site but quickly became exhausted. The most obvious structure is the building
with a semicircular end down by the shore. This was the pan-house or boiling house.
Other ruins and two water-filled mine shafts dot the disturbed ground. On the west
wall of the tiny harbour, facing the sea, are the fossil footprints★ of a 320 million-
year-old giant arthropod called Arthropleura. This cross between a millipede and a
centipede is the largest land-based invertebrate ever known. The tracks, which are

about 2yds (2m) in length, and run parallel to the ground surface, can be hard to make out unless the angle of the sun comes to your aid. There is more on this monster creepy-crawlie from the Carboniferous Age in the ARRAN HERITAGE MUSEUM in Brodick. Some distance further on the path passes a millstone embedded in the ground. The dip between the two hills to the west is Fionn Bhealach, Fingal's Pass (NR981495). You then come to the mighty boulders of The Fallen Rocks, before passing the unusual Blue Cliffs – which are, well, blue – and reaching the end of the route at the North Sannox car park.

SANNOX

From the car park and picnic-site at North Sannox point a Forestry Commission network of paths★ take you to the various burial cairns hidden in the trees. Although no single cairn is truly spectacular, the circular route is worthwhile and is an easy introduction to the 'atmospheric' element of the ruins of chambered cairns. At the start, and just before the forestry fence, is North Sannox Cairn (NS01424659). It is badly mutilated and only one upright stone stands above the vegetation. Back in the nineteenth century it had more than one cist containing human bones, but by the time Prof. Thomas Bryce excavated in 1909 all the contents had long gone. The red way-marked trail leads you to the signposted ('burial cairn') North Sannox Forest Cairn★ (NS01064683). The chamber towards the lower end of the slope is clearly visible. Although badly damaged, the covering of moss and its position in a well-lit clearing surrounded by gloomy forest, gives it a very special ambience. On the return trip from the red route, when going downhill along a straight avenue look out to the right (west) for an unmarked cairn. This is North Sannox Farm Chambered Cairn (NS01114676). Once again the chamber can be seen amidst the scatter of moss-engulfed stones. A short distance south-east is a circular structure, which is probably another cairn, hollowed out and used for some kind of agricultural purpose. Taking the green or blue routes further up the hill takes you to another damaged cairn with a shieling next to it (NS01344669), and at NS01114676 a barely-recognisable D-shaped dun. Note that other than the cairn by the car park none of the monuments are marked on the Ordnance Survey maps.

A short distance back along the road from the car park is a spot called Lag Nan Sasunnach, 'the Englishman's Hollow' or 'the Hollow of the Englishmen' (NS012465). This is supposed to be the grave of some English soldiers killed in a nearby skirmish, presumably the same one that allegedly involved the Cat Stone in CORRIE. A track leads north-west from the road to the pony trekking centre and the ruins of the North Sannox Clearance Settlement. Much of the Sannox area was forcibly cleared in the nineteenth-century, with many tenants emigrating to Canada, the Duke of Hamilton thereby gaining an area for sheep farming that was more profitable than his human tenants (the evictees' story is told in the ARRAN HERITAGE MUSEUM). The most evocative buildings are further west along the path at NS000469, with the corn kiln being particularly striking. A good view of the former settlement can be found from the Iron Age site of the impressive North Sannox Hillfort, uphill to the north-north-west at NS00184738.

Mid Sannox, on the north side of the Sannox Burn, has two fine standing stones★. One (NS01644558) is to the east of the road, in the garden of Dundarroch Cottage,

Mid Sannox standing stone.

immediately south of the lovely early-Victorian North Sannox church. It can easily be seen from the track and is a spectacular 9ft (2.7m) high. The equally-sized second stone (NS01444578) is on a slope to the west of the road, in the grounds of Sannox House, north of the golf clubhouse, and visible from the road about 220yds (200m) north of the bridge over the Sannox Burn. The Ordnance Survey *Name Book* of 1864 states that until the 1830s this was a double circle of tall standing stones, with a single large recumbent slab. When the stones were removed to build a fence, it was this slab that was raised upright, and is the stone that remains. In contrast to this all-too familiar narrative of agricultural destruction of stone circles, in 1863 the then farmer told J. Bryce that there had never been such a circle on the spot, and the standing stone is original.

From the car park south of the burn a path leads west to the popular trek up Glen Sannox. About 220yds (200m) along the first paved path is a graveyard★, site of the now vanished medieval St Michael's Chapel (NS01464528). Many of the older gravestones have toppled or lean crazily. On the north wall, just to the left of the main entrance to the old graveyard (which is surrounded by the newer cemetery) is a crudely-carved face★. This is commonly believed to be St Michael, but it is so eroded that so positive identification is possible. Like the rest of the graveyard, it is protected by a necessary but unsympathetic deer fence. Edwin Rose, the victim of the GOATFELL MURDER, is buried here at Sannox. It is not uncommon to find posies, pebbles and other memorials on Rose's boulder-stone grave.

In an unidentified newspaper cutting of 1957, held by the Arran Heritage Museum, Captain John MacMillan discusses a man called Johnnie Garr: 'In some strange manner he procured all the wealth that he required from a secret spot in Glen Sannox.'

The 'St Michael' carving in Sannox graveyard. The toupee is courtesy of a mat of moss.

The grave of Edwin Rose, victim of the Arran murder, with offerings.

When an old man he was repeatedly asked to reveal the location of the treasure, but always replied that, 'not even his own sons were wise enough to know and that to few men was given the wisdom to handle wealth so easily procured.' There is a spot on the shore midway between Corrie and Sannox called Johnnie Garr's port.

A rocking stone sits on the beach at the south end of South Sannox (NS010449); sadly it no longer rocks. Sannox Chambered Cairn★ (NS01724481) is worth a visit because, although it is ruined, the chamber is clearly visible, there's an upright stone, and it has a great view of the sleeping warrior. Find the seat at the south end of the village, head up the slope and take the stile through the deer fence.

CORRIE

This long, attractive village is home to (with apologies to *The Princess Bride*) several R.O.U.S.'s (Rocks Of Unusual Size). These are either glacial erratics or have tumbled from the heights above. The best example is a short walk north of the village – Clach a' Chath★, the so-called Cat Stone, a massive boulder draped in legend (NS021445). The variants of the basic story are set out in *The Book of Arran 2*. A foraging party of Cromwellian soldiers were on their way back to Brodick Castle when they were ambushed by local people wielding farm tools as weapons. The skirmish started at Allt-a-Chlaidheimh (Sword Burn), north of the stone, and the last trooper was dragged from the shelter of Clach a' Chath. Alternatively, the soldier was found by a local girl at the stone and she hid him until they both managed to escape. Alternatively again, the attack took place near the castle, and the governor and his men escaped in a small boat.

Corrie – the ghost and legend-haunted Clach a' Chath, clearly showing the drill hole.

One man, however, was left behind, and after fleeing for his life was killed under a big rock near the road in the Merkland wood north of the castle. The site was thereafter known as Creag an Stobaidh, the stabbing rock. The location of this particular stone, if it ever existed, is unidentified. There are many variations of this story, with the locations varying from along a considerable stretch of shore, from Brodick to Lag nan Sasunnach (see SANNOX). This may reflect the 'running battle' nature of the fight, or it may be folkloric embroidery. There is no documentary or archaeological evidence for the rammy, but local tradition is persistent on its reality.

The New Statistical Account gives the reason for the attack: the Cromwellian troops 'used some improper liberties with the females of the island, and otherwise conducted themselves with the usual license of conquerors.' The legend may even have influenced the name of the stone: is it Clach a Cath (or Clach a' Chath or Clach a' Chatha), all meaning 'Stone of Battle', or, reflecting its common name of the Cat Stone, is it Clach a' Chait, Stone of the Cat? Or is the latter simply a false retranslation back into Gaelic of the English corruption of the Gaelic original? It's all very confusing. Robert McLellan in his 1985 edition of *The Isle of Arran* discusses a more contemporary battle: 'A recent unauthorised attempt by an employee of the county roads committee to blast a piece off it, in the interests of faster motoring, led to an astonishingly virulent public controversy. The huge stone... bears the scars of the latest conflict in the form of three holes, bored by a pneumatic drill. They will no doubt acquire their own folklore.'

The stone has another, perhaps more supernatural focus. The archive of the Arran Heritage Museum holds a very interesting letter dated 15 July 1996 written by Angus Logan of Langholm to Thomas McFinnie of the museum:

> A ghost is seen occasionally near the Cat Stone. She is the replica of a mother coming in tears from the shore after the naval long boat had carried off her son... one afternoon in early spring as I drew near the Cat Stone, from the Corrie side, I saw an old woman, as I thought coming up from the shore with a grey blanket gathered round her shoulders. What is she doing there, I thought, then she approached the road side, and I saw that her face was ghastly pale, expressionless, as if half asleep. I greeted her, but she made no response, so I continued a few steps further on, intending to turn about to see her from behind, because she was making to cross the road. When I did so, there was no person to be seen. She had vanished. Had I seen the ghost?

Clach an Fhionn, Fingal's Stone★, another unusually-sized rock, is on the north edge of the village, on the east side of the road (NS024440). The largest boulder, Clach Mhor★ (Big Rock), a 62-ton behemoth, is about 110yds (100m) west of the road at the south end of Corrie, just before the treeline (NS025420).

Corrie is also full of other curiosities. Opposite the northernmost harbour a rough, muddy unmarked track leads you to several caves and remains of limestone kilns. Some of the larger caves are used for storage. The Corrie Capers, a week of events at the start of August, ends with the burning of a Viking longboat on Sannox beach. The capstans on the harbours and quays at Corrie (and Sannox) are formed in the shape of sheep. A carved wooden human head sits next to Blackrock in the northern part of the village. Opposite the village shop is a wooden sculpture of a seal lying in a characteristic basking pose, which many people mistake for the real thing. The artist is

Opposite: Wood carving
close to Blackrock, Corrie.

This page top to bottom:
Oviniform capstons; unreal
seal; the Doctor's Bath,
Corrie.

Marvin Elliott, whose work can also be seen in and around the shop (www.sculptor-carver.com). Marvin also reconstructed the face of 'Clachaig Man', from one of the prehistoric skulls found in Claichaig cairn (see ARRAN HERITAGE MUSEUM).

South of the shop is the Doctor's Bath★, a sea-bathing basin dug out of the sandstone rock by a Dr McCredy, who stayed in 'Cromla' in the early nineteenth century. Find Cromla Cottage and go diagonally south across the rocks. The bath has steps leading down into it and is about 12ft (3.6m) long, 6ft (1.8m) wide and 5ft (1.5m) deep, although if you'd want to bathe in it today you'd better like seaweed.

The Fairy Garden, Holy Island.

9

ARRAN AND POPULAR CULTURE

Arran features in a number of mainstream novels (including works by the noted local author Robert McLellan) but here I have concentrated on Arran's role in the more obscure and intriguing byways of popular culture.

The *Star Trek* universe – which now encompasses not just films and television series but a plethora of novels and comic books – has created an entire alternative history. In the episode 'Assignment: Earth', broadcast during the 1968 season of the original television series, the crew of the starship *Enterprise*, on a time-traveling jaunt, encounter a human interplanetary agent called Gary Seven, whose mission is to prevent the people of Earth destroying themselves in a nuclear holocaust. Gary Seven went on to be a character in several *Star Trek* short stories and novels, including *The Eugenics Wars: The Rise And Fall Of Khan Noonien Singh, Volume Two*, by Greg Cox. In that book, on 10 September 1993, following a confrontation in London in which bystanders died, Seven relocated his headquarters to Arran, so as to minimise civilian casualties. And as he has a twenty-third century transporter à la *Star Trek*, he can shop anywhere. The story focuses on his resistance to Khan, a genetically-enhanced tyrant who instigated the world-wide Eugenics Wars on 1990s Earth. Of his new home, Seven noted that Blackwaterfoot 'sounded like something badly translated from Andorian.' Seven is said to have visited Arran first in 1973, investigating 'the mysterious disappearance of a Scottish policeman on a nearby island, which had proved to be home to a blood-thirsty pagan cult' – a puckish reference to the film *The Wicker Man*, released that year, in which Edward Woodward's stolid Presbyterian policeman was burnt alive in a huge wicker effigy, and typical of Cox's fertile pop-culture cross-pollinations. Note that Gary Cox also penned the spoof episode guide to *Vixen the Slayer* which mentions Blackwaterfoot. I think he likes the name.

The comic *TV Century 21* was launched in 1965 as an adjunct to and promotion for Gerry Anderson's science fiction puppet adventure television series such as *Stingray*, *Fireball XL5* and *Thunderbirds*. One of the main colour strips was 'Lady Penelope' (subtitled 'Elegance, Charm and Deadly Danger'), which charted the twenty-first century adventures of two of the minor characters from *Thunderbirds* – the titular glamorous young socialite and her Cockney ex-criminal chauffeur Parker ('Yus, M'Lady'). Issues 35 to 43 featured a story entitled 'The Isle of Arran Mystery', in which Lady P. and Parker, in pursuit of an inheritance, have to solve a series of riddles set by the eccentric late Lord Neddy Clingsdale. Probably written by Tod Sullivan, it displays a detailed knowledge of Arran's topography and legends. The details are on the 'Gerry Anderson Complete Comic History' website (see bibliography).

The first two riddles having identified Arran as the site of the treasure, the third, 'Village, Castle, Bay and String. Under the bed in Western Wing,' clearly refers to Brodick, which has a village, castle and bay, with the String Road leading to it. Under the bed in the western wing of Brodick Castle the pair find the next clue: 'Horns and beard, do not fall, climb to the north and turn the ball.' 'Horns and beard' mean a goat, so the next clue must be on Goatfell. At this point Penelope and Parker are attacked and overtaken by a man called Hawkins, an assassin sent by other seekers after the treasure, so Parker drives FAB 1, Penelope's bullet-proof pink Rolls Royce, to the top of the mountain. Even in the year 2065 this seems unlikely. A ball-shaped boulder on the peak is carved with the next riddle: 'Castle for Robert when on the run, nor'west stands the ruin, facing the gun.' This refers to the unlikely legend that Robert the Bruce visited Lochranza, and in the ruined castle there the duo find the next clue: 'Stand in a circle and look some more, third on the right beside the Tor.' Fending off the trigger-happy Hawkins first with a lighter that turns into an atomic pistol – it fires 'minute atomic capsules with regulated safe fall-out' – and then, shades of James Bond, via a car-to-car tyre shredder, Parker and her ladyship drive FAB 1 to the stone circles on Machrie Moor, also known as Tormore. At the stone circle (which one is not mentioned) the third stone on the right holds the next clue: 'Light for the Firth, now facing South. Go to the edge and 'ware seal's mouth.' This is the island of Pladda, on which is a lighthouse for the Firth of Clyde. FAB 1 is sabotaged by Hawkins. Despite Lady Penelope hiring a fishing boat from Lagg Inn, Hawkins gets to the island first, and finds the clue in the skull of a seal on the beach: 'Black, bare and Royal, kept so spruce, now up again to the lie of Bruce.' With FAB 1 repaired by the AA – who arrive via helicopter - Parker and Penelope follow the killer to the King's Cave (supposedly where Robert the Bruce stayed in 1307). They overcome Hawkins and discover another clue etched on the cave wall: 'Legend you know of a long dead king. Lash has a hill where you'll find a ring.' 'Lash' must be Lamlash, where supposedly RTB encountered the never-say-die spider. In the stone circle at the top of Lamlash hill Parker and Penelope dig under the central stone and find the treasure – a ruby ring worth half a million pounds. Great fun, although the practice of carving cryptic messages on historic sites should not be encouraged. Even if you are an eccentric millionaire aristocrat.

Detail of gravestone, Kilbride church, Lamlash.

BIBLIOGRAPHY

Works which have been of especial use are marked with an asterisk★.

NEWSPAPERS

Ardrossan & Saltcoats Herald:
Undated: 'Old Arran – Forgotten Tales' by Malcolm Sillars. Original in Isle of Arran
 Heritage Museum Archive, shelfmark ARNM 45/9.6
  30 May 1884: Ailsa Craig – graves found
  27 November 1896: 'A Legend of the Holy Isle' by 'A.B.C.'
  12 February 1897: Lochranza ghost
Ayr Observer:
  4 June 1844: report on the start of the rebuilding of Brodick Castle
The Scotsman:
  2 February 2006: 'UFOs over West Kilbride' by Sarah Roe

HISTORY, ARCHAEOLOGY AND RELIGION – ARRAN

[No author] *Tales from Scottish Lairds* Jarrold Colour Publications, Norwich 1985
Arran Heritage Community Group *Isle of Arran Heritage: The Arran High School Project*
 (Arran Heritage Community Group; Arran, 2002)★
Balfour, J.A. 'The Ecclesiastical Remains on the Holy Isle, Arran' in *Proceedings of the
 Society of Antiquaries of Scotland,* Vol. 43, 1908–09
Balfour, J.A. (ed) *The Book of Arran Volume 1: Archaeology* (Kilbrannan Publishing;
 Brodick, 1982) (first published 1910)★
Bryce, James 'An Account of Excavations within the Stone Circles of Arran' in
 Proceedings of the Society of Antiquaries of Scotland, Vol. 4, 1860–2
Bussell, Gillean *Arran: Behind the Scenes* (Arran Graphics; Arran, 1999)
Cameron, Kennedy *The Church in Arran* (John Grant; Edinburgh, 1912)
Currie, Ronald *The Place-Names of Arran* (The Banton Press; Isle of Arran, 2002) (first
 published 1908)
Fairhurst, Horace *Exploring Arran's Past* (Kilbrannan Publishing; Brodick, 1982)★
Fforde, Lady Jean *Castles in the Air* (Kilbrannan Publishing; Brodick, 1982)
Gemmell, Alastair *Discovering Arran* (John Donald; Edinburgh, 1990)
Haggarty, Alison 'Machrie Moor' in *Current Archaeology*, Vol. 109, April 1988
 ——————— 'Machrie Moor, Arran: recent excavations at two stone circles' in
 Proceedings of the Society of Antiquaries of Scotland, Vol. 121, 1991

Hartley, Christopher, John Basford, Derrick Warner and John Forgie *Brodick Castle, Country Park and Goatfell* (The National Trust for Scotland; Edinburgh, 2006)

Headrick, Revd James *View of the Minerology, Agriculture, Manufacturies and Fisheries of the Island of Arran, with Notices of Antiquities and Suggestions for Improving the Agriculture and Fisheries of the Highlands and Islands of Scotland* (Constable; Edinburgh, 1807)

Isle of Arran Heritage Museum Guide Book (The Isle of Arran Heritage Museum; Brodick, 2007)

Janson, Kristine *Holy Island* (Karma Drubgyud Darjay Ling; Kagyu Samye Ling Monastery, Eskadalemuir, 2007)★

Kenny, Colum *Molaise: Abbot of Leighlin and Hermit of Holy Island* (Morrigan Books; Killala, Co Mayo, 1998)

McArthur, John *The Antiquities of Arran with a Historical Sketch of the Island* (Adam and Charles Black; Edinburgh, 1873) (first published 1861)★

——————— 'On the rude unsculptured monoliths, and ancient fortifications of the island of Arran' in *Edinburgh New Philosophical Journal*, Vol. 9, 1859

MacBride, Mackenzie *Arran of the Bens the Glens and the Brave* (T.N. Foulis; London and Edinburgh, 1911)

MacKenzie, W.M. (ed) *The Book of Arran Volume 2: History and Folklore* (Kilbrannan Publishing; Brodick, 1982) (first published 1914)★

McKerrell, Hugh *Isle of Arran – Walking the Past* no date or publisher★

McLaughlin, Bill *Molaise of Arran: A Saint of the Celtic Church* (W.J. McLaughlin; Isle of Arran, 1999)★

McLellan, Robert *The Isle of Arran* (David & Charles; Newton Abbot and London, 1985) (first published 1970)★

McLellan, Robert (revised Norman Newton) *The Isle of Arran* (Pevensey Press; Newton Abbot, 1995)

McLellan, Robert, Gordon Barclay & Christopher Tabraham *The Ancient Monuments of Arran* (Historic Scotland; Edinburgh, 1989)★

MacMillan, Captain John 'Memories of Arran', unidentified newspaper cutting dated 3 February 1957, in Isle of Arran Heritage Museum Archive, shelfmark ARNM 4498.6

Meighan, Ian and Derek Simpson 'Machrie Moor Stone Circles' in *Current Archaeology* No. 176 October/November 2001

Milne, Allan Paterson *Arran: An Island's Story* (Kilbrannan Publishing; Brodick, 1982)

Mitchell, Alison (ed) *Pre-1855 Gravestone Inscriptions in Bute and Arran* (Scottish Genealogy Society; Edinburgh, 1987)

New Statistical Account 'Parish of Kilbride' and 'Parish of Kilmorie', Vol. V, (William Blackwood; Edinburgh, 1845)

Richards, Colin 'The Great Stone Circles Project' in *British Archaeology* No. 81 March/ April 2005

Roughead, William (ed.) *Trial of John Watson Laurie (The Arran Murder)* (William Hodge & Co.; Edinburgh and London, 1932)

Scott, A Boyd *The East of Arran: A Guide-Book for the Young of All Ages* (The Banton Press; Isle of Arran, 1995) (first published 1919)

Thompson, Ruth and Alan *The Milestones of Arran* (no publisher; Lamlash, 2000)

Whyte, Hamish (ed) *An Arran Anthology* (Mercat Press; Edinburgh, 1997)★

Wilson, Daniel 'Holy Island, and the Runic Inscriptions of St Molio's Cave, County of Bute' in *Proceedings of the Society of Antiquaries of Scotland*, Vol. 17, 1882-83

UNPUBLISHED WORKS

Logan, Angus - untitled letter to Thomas McFinnie 15 July 1996, in Isle of Arran Heritage Museum Archive, shelf mark ARNM 2962.2

Stewart, Donald 'Echoes of the Old Time Ceildih: address to the Arran Ceilidh, 11 November 1924', typescript in Isle of Arran Heritage Museum Archive, shelfmark ARNM 542

———————— 'Postman's Journey', 1937, typescript in Isle of Arran Heritage Museum Archive, shelfmark ARNM 543

HISTORY AND ARCHAEOLOGY – SCOTLAND AND UK

Allen, J. Romilly and Joseph Anderson, *The Early Christian Monuments of Scotland*, Vol. 2, Part 3 (The Pinkfoot Press; Forfar, 1993) (originally published 1903)

Barnett, John 'Monuments in the Landscape: Thoughts from the Peak' in Alex Gibson and Derek Simpson (eds) *Prehistoric Ritual and Religion* (Sutton Publishing; Stroud, 1998)

Barbour, John *The Bruce* (Canongate Books; Edinburgh, 1998)

Burl, Aubrey *The Stone Circles of the British Isles* Yale (University Press; New Haven and London, 1976)

———————— *Rings of Stone: The prehistoric stone circles of Britain and Ireland* (Frances Lincoln; London, 1979)

———————— *Rites of the Gods* (J.M. Dent & Sons; London, 1981)

———————— *The Stone Circles of Britain, Ireland and Brittany* (Yale University Press; New Haven and London, 1995)

Chalmers, Robert *Domestic Annals of Scotland - From the Reformation to the Revolution* (W. & R. Chambers; Edinburgh and London, 1874)

Fisher, Ian *Early Medieval Sculpture in the West Highlands and Islands* (RCAHMS and the Society of Antiquaries of Scotland; Edinburgh, 2001)★

Haswell-Smith, Hamish *The Scottish Islands* (Canongate; Edinburgh, 1996)

Hayman, Richard *Riddles in Stone: Myths, Archaeology and the Ancient Britons* (The Hambledon Press; London, 1997)

Henshall, A.S. *The Chambered Tombs of Scotland* Vol. 2 (Edinburgh University Press; Edinburgh, 1972)

Martin, Martin *A Description of the Western Islands of Scotland circa 1695,* (Birlinn; Edinburgh, 1994) (first published 1698)★

Millar, W.J. *The Clyde: From Its Source to The Sea* (Blackie; London, 1888)

Mitchell, Sir Arthur 'James Robertson's Tour through some of the Western Islands, etc., of Scotland in 1768' in *Proceedings of the Society of Antiquaries of Scotland*, Vol. 32, 1897-98★

Munro, Sir Donald *A Description of the Western Isles of Scotland Called Hybrides* (Birlinn; Edinburgh, 1994) (first published 1774)

Pennant, Thomas *A Tour in Scotland and Voyage to the Hebrides, 1772* (Birlinn; Edinburgh, 1998) (first published 1776)★

Pórdarson, Sturla (trans by Revd James Johnstone) *The Norwegian Account of Haco's Expedition Against Scotland, 1263* (William Brown; Edinburgh, 1882) (originally published 1782)

Roughead, William *Twelve Scots Trials* (Mercat Press; Edinburgh, 1995) (first published 1913)

Shetelig, Haakon, 'The Viking Graves' in Shetelig, Haakon (ed), *Viking Antiquities in Great Britain and Ireland, Part VI* (H. Aschehoug & Co.; Oslo, 1954)

Steer, K.A. and W.M. Bannerman *Late Medieval Sculpture in the West Highlands* (Royal Commission on Ancient and Historical Monuments in Scotland; Edinburgh 1977)★

Tranter, Nigel *The Queen's Scotland: Argyll and Bute* (Hodder and Stoughton; London, 1977)

WILLIAM BECKFORD

Alexander, Boyd *England's Wealthiest Son: A Study of William Beckford* (Centaur Press; London, 1962)★

Baker, Malcolm, Timothy Schroder & E. Laird Clowes *Beckford and Hamilton Silver from Brodick Castle* (Exhibition Catalogue) (Spink & Son; London, 1980)

Beckford, William *Vathek,* in Peter Fairclough (ed.) *Three Gothic Novels* (Penguin; Harmondsworth, 1986)★

Birkhead, Edith *The Tale of Terror: A Study of the Gothic Romance* (Constable; London, 1921)

Clute, John and John Grant (eds) *The Encyclopedia of Fantasy* (Orbit; London, 1997)

Dejardin, Ian *William Beckford 1760-1844: An Eye for the Magnificent. A Companion to the Exhibition at Dulwich Picture Gallery: 6 February – 14 April 2002* (Gli Ori; London, 2002)

Fothergill, Brian *Beckford of Fonthill* (Faber & Faber; London, 1979)★

Lees-Milne, James *William Beckford* (Compton Russell; Tisbury, 1976)★

Strong, Roy *Lost Treasures of Britain* (Guild Publishing; London, 1990)★

Woodward, Christopher *In Ruins* (Vintage; London, 2002)

MYSTERIOUSNESS

Burt, Bill 'Embraced by Angels', online at www.newfrontier.com/2/angel-story.htm

Campbell, John Gregerson (ed. Ronald Black), *The Gaelic Otherworld: John Gregerson Campbell's Superstitions of the Highlands and Islands of Scotland* and *Witchcraft and Second Sight in the Highlands & Islands* (Birlinn; Edinburgh, new edition 2005) (first published 1900 & 1902)

Carmichael, Alexander (ed. C.J. Moore) *Carmina Gadelica* (Floris Books; Edinburgh, 1994) (first published 1900)

Coventry, Martin *Haunted Castles & Houses of Scotland* (Goblinshed; Musselburgh, 2004)

Doorly, Moyra 'An Invitation to Elfland' in *Fortean Times* No. 179, January 2004★

Hall, Alaric 'Getting Shot of Elves: Healing, Witchcraft and Fairies in the Scottish Witchcraft Trials' in *Folklore*, Vol. 116, 2005

Love, Dane *Scottish Spectres* (Robert Hale; London, 2001)

MacKinlay, James M. *Folklore of Scottish Lochs and Springs* (William Hodge; Glasgow, 1893)

MacLagan, R.C. *Evil Eye in the Western Highlands* (David Nutt; London, 1902)

MacLeod, Fiona (William Sharp) *The Silence of Amor & Where the Forest Murmurs* (Duffield & Co.; New York, 1911)

——————————— The Winged Destiny & Studies In The Spiritual History Of The Gael (Heinemann; London, 1913)

MacPhail, Malcolm 'Folklore from the Hebrides IV' in Folklore, Vol. 11, No. 4, December 1900

Napier, James Folk Lore, or Superstitious Beliefs in the West of Scotland Within This Century (Alex. Gardner; Paisley, 1879)

Sherbourne, Grahame 'The Wizard of the Ancient World' in Northern Earth 75 online at www.northernearth.co.uk

Tame, David Real Fairies: True Accounts of Meetings with Nature Spirits (Capall Bann; Chieveley, 1999)

Thompson, Francis The Supernatural Highlands (Luath Press; Edinburgh, 1997)

Underwood, Peter Gazetteer of Scottish Ghosts (Fontana/Collins, Glasgow, 1975)

——————————— This Haunted Isle (Harrap; London, 1984)

FICTION

Cox, Greg The Eugenics Wars: The Rise And Fall Of Khan Noonien Singh, Volume Two (Pocket Books; New York, 2003)

Edghill, Rosemary The Warslayer; An Incredibly True Adventure Of Vixen The Slayer, The Beginning (Baen Books; New York, 2002)

Scott, Sir Walter The Lord of the Isles (International Law and Taxational Publishers; 2002) (first published 1815)

WEBSITES

'Canmore' – Royal Commission on Ancient and Historic Monuments in Scotland: www.rcahms.gov.uk★

The Encyclopedia of Speculative Fiction:http://encyclopedia.wizards.pro/index. php/Main_Page

The Gerry Anderson Complete Comic History: www.technodelic.pwp.blueyonder co.uk★

Memory Alpha, the Star Trek encyclopaedia: http://memory-alpha.org/en/wiki/ Portal:Main

The Modern Antiquarian: www.modernantiquarian★

Northern Earth magazine: www.northernearth.co.uk

The Sites and Monuments Record of the West of Scotland Archaeology Service: www.wosas.org.uk★

INDEX

Other local titles published by The History Press

The Guide to Mysterious Iona and Staffa
GEOFF HOLDER

This is a guide to everything supernatural, paranormal, folkloric, eccentric and, above all, mysterious about the island of Iona and the nearby island of Staffa. Containing fairies and martyrs, Celtic gods, telepathy, exorcism and magic, druids, witches, mermaids, demons and saints (and based on texts both ancient and modern), it is a fascinating introduction to the islands' heritage.

978 07524 4380 5

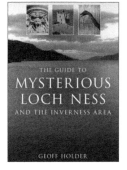

The Guide to Mysterious Loch Ness and the Inverness Area
GEOFF HOLDER

This is a guide to everything mysterious that has occured by the dark waters of Loch Ness and the surrounding area. With sections on big cats, second sight, the exorcism of the Lock, folk magic, fairies, UFOs and, of course, the strange history of the Loch's most famous resident, this is a fascinating introduction to the heritage of this spectacular part of Scotland.

978 07524 4385 7

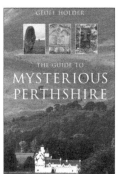

The Guide to Mysterious Perthshire
GEOFF HOLDER

This guide is a fascinating introduction to Perthshire's tombstones, simulacra, standing stones, gargoyles and archaeological curiosities. There are tales of ghosts, fairies, witchcraft, freak weather, strange deaths, tall tales and hoaxes. It is profusely illustrated with the author's own photographs and there are extensive references and endnotes to enable the reader to follow up the sources, if he should so wish.

978 07524 4140 5

Haunted Edinburgh
ALAN MURDIE

Explore the darkest secrets of Edinburgh's past with this collection of stories, telling of the inexplicable occurrences and ghostly apparitions that have haunted residents of the city over the centuries. Compiled by the former chairman of the Ghost Club and illustrated with more than seventy images from his own collection, this book is sure to capture the imagination of any reader with an interest in the paranormal history of the city.

978 07524 4356 9